LOW AND SLOW

A personal history of a Liaison Pilot in World War II

by Don Moore

San Antonio Heights Publishing Company
Upland, California

Published by:
San Antonio Heights Publishing Company
P. O. Box 571
Upland, CA 91785-057

TABLE OF CONTENTS

TABLE OF CONTENTS Continued

Foreword

This is the story of a courageous group of men and their romance with the sky....of men who flew it in combat armed only with a pistol....of men who attacked the enemy on all fronts with aircraft made of tubing, wires and fabric.

Donald Moore's account of his and their deeds has made possible the following book sharing with us their experiences.

The common denominator of the Liaison Pilots and their Liaison aircraft is their love of heritage, their desire to preserve that heritage and to make their unheralded experiences and histories available to the unknowing public.

No one shows this dedication more than my dear friend, Don Moore, with this book. Enjoy!

William Stratton, President,
International Liaison Pilot and Aircraft Association

Preface

The expression "low and slow" comes from a standard joke among cadet pilots. Someone's mother said: "Son, be careful; fly low and slow." Now, "low and slow" makes your instructor pull out his hair. He insists that you maintain sufficient altitude to complete the maneuvers you wish to do. He wants you to add a huge safety margin, including consideration for Federal Aviation Administration (FAA) and military regulations concerning low flights over populated areas. He will tell you: "The air above you does you no good; only that below you is available for recovery from a maneuver or from an emergency." He will rail against slow flight just as strongly. "Maintain your air speed at all times; stalling speed plus fifty percent on approach. Especially when you are forced to fly low, as on approach, keep up your airspeed!" The Liaison Pilot training and rating that we received prepared us, nevertheless, to ignore these warnings.

In World War II, and later in the Korean War, some Army Artillery officers were trained to fly civilian type light aircraft. The motive of the War Department to do this came from the experience of two famous WWII generals. The reasoning and the arguments for this type of training for officers not in the Army Air Corps will be described in Chapter 1. The Army Air Corps (forerunner of the Air Force) had a rating called Liaison Pilot. These pilots did not receive training in the high performance military aircraft of the day, nor even in the intermediate and advanced training planes used by the Air Corps. Rather, they were trained in light, fabric covered, generally two-place aircraft like those used for civilian pilot training and sport applications in that day. We are talking about the late

1930's and early 1940's. The term liaison meant the same as the dictionary definition of the term: "(1) An instance or means of communication between bodies, groups or units, (2) a. A close relationship..." We'll skip the (2) b offering in the American Heritage Dictionary of the English Language, 1976 edition. It is: "b. An adulterous relationship."

The Air Corps cadets who were trained as Liaison Pilots did perform largely liaison functions. It was essential that the armed forces have their own capability of providing rapid transportation of commanding officers, medical personnel and officers assigned to a true liaison function between units of the Air Corps, or between Air Corps and ground units, or between Air Corps and units of the Navy or Marines. This transportation and messenger function was very important. Yet, because of the lesser training given to these pilots, they were given the rank of Staff Sergeant. This is an "E-5" rank on the pay scale, while the scale for enlisted personnel goes to "E-9." On the other hand, the Table of Organization position of Liaison Pilot in the Army Artillery called for a rank of First Lieutenant, "O-2" on the officer pay scale. The discrepancy can be rationalized by noting that the primary occupational specialty of the Army ground forces Liaison Pilot was Artillery Officer, and flying was only a secondary specialty. In the Army Artillery, after World War II, a four-place, all metal, complex aircraft was acquired. This, called the L-17, was the same as the civilian Navion by North American. It had little tactical utility, and we dubbed it "the General's Jeep." It performed a truly liaison function, along with pilot assigned to fly it on any given day. Two-place non-complex aircraft were still used for tactical jobs, principally the observation and spotting functions of the

Artillery, in support of Infantry.

When the Army was authorized to have pilots on the Table of Organization of Artillery battalions, the obvious source of training for them was the Air Corps. The pilot rating that seemed to fit was that of Liaison Pilot. Therefore, Artillery officers were shipped off to two training locations, one in Manhattan, Kansas, and one in Denton, Texas. The one in Denton used the facilities of the North Texas State College for classrooms and dormitories, and a turf field north of town for flight training. The facility in Manhattan also used the resources of a State College. Civilian instructors were employed, giving the student pilot 60 hours of flight instruction. This is about what it takes to prepare a student for the Private Pilot Certificate. The rest of the training was given at the Artillery School at Fort Sill, Oklahoma, as described in Chapter 1. Actually, much of what we learned that enabled us to perform our mission and stay alive was learned in the field after we were assigned to an Artillery battalion.

What follows is the personal story of one such Artillery officer who opted for the flight training and consequent duty in training and in combat. The story does not pretend to be a history of a campaign, but rather it is a series of stories about flying under the conditions that we encountered, with all of the stresses, failures and successes that went with such duty. As you will see, we certainly were not heroes. Neither were we cowards. We attempted to stay alive, yet we performed as we were expected to perform. A few lost their lives. So did a lot of other people.

My debts of gratitude are many. For the inspiration to do this work, I owe Alfred "Dutch" Schultz, Kirk Neff and John Kriegsman. For help in locating information and

Civilian instructor Lloyd Nalen, former crop duster, is in the center. His four students included the author, right.

recalling events I owe much to Professor Emeritus (formerly Captain) Robert Munyon, Ken Camozzi, Major General (Ret.) James Delk, Paul Armstrong, Bill Stratton, John Kriegsman, Sam Sammons, the staff at the Upland public library and the staff at Headquarters, 40th Infantry Division (M), California Army National Guard, especially Sergeant Jones, Major Bernd Willand and Major General Zysk.

For help in editing, I want to express my gratitude to my cousin Lee Hatch, to that former English teacher Wesley Blasjo and to my patient wife Kathleen, the world's best proof reader.

Chapter One

WHY WE FLEW LOW AND SLOW

This is a story of how the Pacific part of World War II appeared to a Lieutenant of Artillery who was a Liaison Pilot. Most of the experiences were in the Philippines, as that was the site of two of the principal campaigns of the 40th Infantry Division, to which the author belonged. There was a relatively quiet period of service on New Britain Island, just north of New Guinea. There was a brief period, after the end of the war, in which the Division served as occupation troops in South Korea. All of this will be covered.

It is a personal story, attempting to give the reader a sense of what it was like to be an amateur soldier and a newly trained pilot of light aircraft in that conflict. Some of the stories have their amusing aspect. Some are sardonic. Some are exciting. Some are dull. That is the way the war was. I have relied on histories to get some data and dates straight. All that I tell is from memory, except when I quote a fellow Liaison Pilot who had quite a different experience.

Our first flight instructors had taught us the dangers of flying too low and slow. Yet, in the Army Artillery, you find perfectly intelligent junior officers with aviation ratings, carrying other officers as observers, flying low and slow over target areas. The Artillery School at Fort Sill, Oklahoma taught them to do so in three weeks of "tactical flying" training given them after completing primary courses in Denton, Texas or Manhattan, Kansas, to earn the Liaison Pilot rating..

The airplanes we used were selected with the "low and slow" capability in mind. Also, maintenance in the field, with the simplest of tools and supplies was a consideration. Consolidated Vultee produced a two-place fabric covered airplane designated the Liaison One (L-1). It was larger and more powerful than necessary, and hard to maintain in the field. It was used a great deal in the China-Burma-India theater, where Liaison squadrons were particularly effective. Taylorcraft modified its civilian aircraft to become the L-2, and Aeronca did likewise to supply the L-3. The most popular turned out to be the Piper Cub, the most widely used training aircraft of the time, and it became the L-4. Consolidated Vultee modified an old Stinson model to produce the L-5. All of these were two-place, single engine, fixed landing gear aircraft, and relatively simple to maintain in rough field conditions. The L-2, L-3 and L-4 all had 65 horsepower engines, no electrical systems, and had to be "hand propped" to start the engine. The L-5 had 185 hp, an electrical system, and many of them had a side opening so that a patient on a stretcher could be carried when the back seat was folded down. Interstate Aircraft modified its 65 horsepower Interstate Cadet to become the L-6 with a "greenhouse" and a 90 horsepower engine. The "greenhouse" is a Plexiglas cabin with sides sloping outward, so that the observer or pilot may look straight down while the wings of the airplane are level.

I weighed 135 pounds. The L-4 weighed 680 pounds, empty.

Why were we Artillery officers, and why were we integrated with Artillery battalions? During the period of the United States preparation for possible involvement in the war, the observation function of aviation received little attention. Yet ground force commanders felt the need for closely coordinated aerial observation. Here I cite William Stratton:[1]

"While few Air Corps procurement military geniuses were ready to concede it, the answer to the ground commanders' complaints was already at hand in the form of the small, easily maintained light planes that were being produced and sold by the hundreds all around America: Aeroncas, Pipers, Taylorcrafts, Porterfields, and Rearwins flew with a third of the horsepower of the PT-17 Stearman that was the Air Corps' primary trainer. They could also operate at a quarter of the cost. The average hot-shot Air Corps pilot was accustomed to big, fast and sophisticated war planes and hardly considered the light craft airplanes at all. On the other hand, many ground officers had learned to fly as a hobby and so they began to consider seriously the role of the light plane in combat.

"With war clouds rising over Europe, the fall of Poland and the expansion of Hitler in 1939 and 1940, the United States was forced to step up its plans to rearm.

"President Roosevelt called for the production of 50,000 planes a year. In May 1940, executives of the aviation industry were called to a Presidential conference in Washington, D. C., where detailed outlines and elaborate plans were presented and discussed. As the meeting wound down, light plane representatives realized they had been left completely out of all the discussions. ...Ed Porterfield spoke first: 'General, will there be any place in this program for light planes?' 'No, at least not in the Army Air Corps. They are impractical for military use.' 'Then how about the Navy?' 'I'm afraid not.' Was the answer from a Navy Captain.

"William Piper, Sr. stood up and said sternly: 'It seems to me that the light plane has not been given a chance to show what it can do. Now that we are here, we would like to explain our side of the story to somebody, anybody: a sergeant or corporal, maybe.'

"Laughter filled the room, then the light plane manufacturers were brushed off with the advice that there would be no military light planes at that time: a grim introduction to the defense policy for the light plane builders."

Both General Eisenhower and General Patton (before they were Generals), while directing troops in Louisiana maneuvers before we were in the war, learned to be private pilots. They rented light aircraft such as the Cub to get better views of the action. They were able to convince the Pentagon of the usefulness of this type of integrated observation capability. Thus the initial reluctance to use light aircraft was dispelled. Piper, Taylorcraft, Aeronca and Consolidated Vultee were given contracts to produce aircraft for the Army, the airplanes to be used by the Artillery branch, not the Air Corps. They determined that the use of non-com Liaison pilots trained by the Air Force alone would be less effective than having officers who knew artillery tactics trained as pilots.

All of these aircraft were good at slow flight, and could be flown in and out of very short fields, or fields with trees or hills as barriers to either end. They could be and were flown off roads, beaches and even small ships. (More of that "carrier" flying will be told later.) The L-4 was particularly good at slow flight, as its stalling speed was 38 mph, with a 70 mph cruise speed. Heading into the wind, it could almost hover, or at least proceed across a target area so slowly that an observer could get

5

a prolonged view of a target or a suspicious movement to be observed. It was relatively safe to "fly low," too. It gave plenty of warning before stalling by shuddering, and recovery from a stall could be achieved with little altitude loss. There were few slow flying accidents with the L-4.

I had an additional advantage in that my first instructor was formerly a crop duster pilot. After our lesson, he would show me some tricks used in that profession, such as making low turns, flying under wires, landing in awkward places, and other things not exactly approved by the FAA.

My friend and fellow Artilleryman "Dutch" Schultz reports that, in North Africa and Europe, he chose 800 feet above the terrain as his flight level. It was above ground fire and hard for anti-aircraft fire and enemy fighters to target.[2] Our terrain in the Pacific was usually volcanic islands, so that the terrain had many slopes to it. I suppose that 800 feet was a good guess at the average height above the terrain that we preferred, but we were always climbing and descending around the mountains.

The story that I am telling in this volume is largely that of the recapture of Luzon and two islands of the Visayan Group in the Philippines in World War II. All of the action occurred between January and August, 1945. There is a prologue, in Chapter 3, describing a stay in the South Pacific. There is a chapter which speaks briefly about our stay in South Korea at the end of World War II. There our task was to ship all Japanese civilians and military personnel back to Japan and to keep the lid on the political pot while it boiled. There were many political parties and factions among the Koreans. They had had no self rule at all under the Japanese for 35 years, so there was little experience on the part of the Koreans. They certainly did not lack enthusiasm. I personally got little experience in the government of South Korea, for I was a technician, flying people, messages and medicines around the peninsula.

Chapter Two

WAR IS INDEED HELL

Few Americans, be they leading literary lights or public figures, have been quoted more frequently than has General William Tecumseh Sherman. In response to criticism of his treatment of Georgia, he said: "War is hell." War really is hell, as every veteran of real battles will agree. In particular, there is now, 50 some years later, the re-telling of events in World War II, to counteract the glamorized versions shown in 50 years of movies. The 1998 movie, "Saving Private Ryan," is one such re-telling. A number of stories and movies about the Vietnam war did not wait 50 years to tell the grim truth. The characterization rings true about the campaigns and battles of WWII fought in the Pacific as well. I have just read Don Richter's "Where the Sun Stood Still," a narrative of the battle for Guadalcanal. This was hell on wheels, and the number of dead was appalling. Fortunately for us, the vast majority of the dead were Japanese, but U. S. Marines, Navy, Army and Air Corps service men experienced the same hell of war.

I suppose that any hell has to have its devil or devils. The Japanese enemy played that role, shall we say, magnificently? They were, to us, "the Jap," and much despised. This was partly because, in any war, the enemy must be demonized in order for the fighting forces to do to them what needs to be done. On the other hand, what we learned from experience and from narratives by Filipinos and others subjected to their rule seemed to justify our contempt. My apologies to the fine Japanese citizens and Japanese Americans I have known, but these were different days and different circumstances. The Japanese military forces were in the grip of an early medieval type of rule and indoctrination which made them into a robotic fighting machine. The remarkable thing, at the end of the war, was to see how happily the surviving Japanese soldier or airman forgot his indoctrination and wanted to learn to speak and read English.

The stories that I tell here are mainly about a part of the task of re-taking the Philippines, which must have been hell for the Infantry, Armored, Paratroops and others on the line. The war observed from 800 or so feet in the air, however, was a funky sort of hell. We saw, from our altitudes, a good deal of the action, but at a distance that allowed us to think of it as unreal, or happening in slow motion. It was real, and it happened in real time.

People have asked me since: "Were you not awfully exposed, up there in that fabric airplane?" My answer is, "Yes, but not as exposed as those I saw on the ground. I developed evasive flying tactics which must have worked, for I was never hit. People on the ground were hit." Let me cite two examples.

One day I flew a new Second Lieutenant, a replacement fresh from the United States, on an Artillery mission. All of this was new to him, and he was scared, but he performed his best. All junior Artillery officers must at some time serve as forward observers (F. O. s) on the ground. They go up with the most forward elements of the Infantry and establish observation posts in places where they have a good view of the target area. The enemy usually, therefore, has a good view of the location of the F. O. The radio technology of the day required a long antenna in order to reach the fire direction center with the field radio. That long antenna was often their undoing. It became a primary target for the enemy, for they knew what was the mission of the F. O. The young lieutenant, whom I did not really get to know, and whom I had not remembered until reaching this point in this story, went on his first F. O. mission a few days after his flight with me. He took one bullet through the head, and that was the end.

Another example was an experienced Lieutenant, an ex football player, business owner and National Guard officer. He was as outgoing and confident as anyone in his outfit. "Big Red," as he was called, seemed to be free of being "nervous in the service," as we termed those who showed their fright at being shot at. He was on F. O. duty and was pinned in his foxhole for 36 hours.

He could not raise his head, get out and relieve himself, or get food or water. The enemy fired shots, at irregular intervals, across the top of his foxhole. When a team reached him, he was a trembling, mumbling creature who could not communicate with his rescuers. In World War I this was called "shell shock" and in WWII it was called "battle fatigue," and there were better techniques for treating it. I hope that there were effective treatments for him. He was hospitalized, and he may have been returned to duty, but I doubt it, for I never saw him again, and he was hard to miss in a crowd. He was bigger than anyone else, and louder. I have often wondered what really was the fate of Big Red.

These examples show you that those who were flying were fortunate, and that the hell that we experienced from the air was more funky than demonic. There is a 1985 book called "Box Seat Over Hell," by Hardy D. Cannon,[3] with research by my friend Bill Stratton, President of the International Liaison Pilot and Airplane Association. Cannon describes the various conditions under which Liaison planes were flown in the several theaters of World War II. The hell they observed below them almost always was worse than they were experiencing. However, those flights could be interesting. In this volume you will read about some flights that appear to be dull; yet a pilot never knew when hours of routine flying were to be interrupted by extremely interesting events. Once some wag or jaded pilot defined flying as hours of boredom interrupted by moments of stark terror. To me, that is the way the war appeared to be. The days were unbelievably boring. Some of the flights were quite dull. Then there were the, shall we say, interesting portions of the flights.

Chapter Three

A HOLDING
PATTERN IN THE
SOUTH PACIFIC

After six months of teaching officer candidates in the Artillery School following my graduation from the same, I applied for flight training and went through the primary course in Denton, Texas. Then there was tactical training at Fort Sill. I was then assigned to a unit in Fort Lewis Washington, and later shipped to the Pacific through Fort Ord California as a casual officer. A casual officer was not a part of any unit; he was to be assigned as a replacement to some unit after arrival in the theater. We were a miscellaneous group of replacement troops, sailing on a troop ship of the General class. These were built by Kaiser Ship Building, and were similar to their "Liberty Ships" that were built as freighters. These were designed to carry troops, and were named for past generals of our Army and Marines. I have forgotten the name of the General honored by our ship. It did not have a long life and is long since forgotten. It was torpedoed and sunk on the

15

way back to the U. S., while carrying sick and wounded service persons. I did not learn the number of casualties there were in that sinking. The ship's speed was eight knots. The course was subject to a "zig" or a "zag" at intervals that varied in length, to confuse any lurking submarines. These factors explain the long time it took to go from San Francisco to Lae, New Guinea, with stops at New Caledonia and Port Moresby, in Papua, New Guinea. (It took forty-four days.)

This is at Lae, New Guinea. The man in the middle is a now unidentified friend. The others are from Shelton, Washington (population about 3,000 in 1944). On the left is Captain Paul Armstrong, later to help inspect the 40th Division for readiness to invade Japan. Next is the author. On the right are Sgt. Will Jackson and Cpl. Bill Mallows.

After a wait in Lae, New Guinea in a replacement depot (called a "repple depple"), I was sent to the 40th Infantry Division located on New Britain Island. The

40th Infantry Division was and is a National Guard Division, with units in Southern California, Utah, Nevada and Arizona. The Division had defended the outer islands of Hawaii from July 1942 to January, 1943. After a short time on Oahu, they went to Guadalcanal in December of 1943 and to New Britain in April of 1944. I joined them in July, 1944. New Britain is a long island stretching northeast and southwest just north of New Guinea, a much bigger island. Eastern New Guinea, called Papua, and New Britain were governed by Australia.

Each Infantry Division had three Infantry regiments, with an artillery battalion (light artillery, 105 MM howitzers) supporting each one, and one battalion of medium, or 155 mm howitzers in general support. The 40th Infantry consisted of the 108th , the 160th, and the 185th Infantry Regiments. They were supported by the 143rd, the 164th and the 213th Field Artillery Battalions, all light artillery plus the 222nd Field Artillery Battalion, medium artillery. There were, of course, Combat Engineer units, Signal Corps, Quartermaster, Ordinance, Medical and Judge Advocate General units in the Division.

Division artillery consisted of the four Artillery Battalions plus a Headquarters Battery and a Service Battery. Each battalion was assigned two Lieutenant pilots and two L-4s. Division Artillery Headquarters had two L-4s, a Lieutenant pilot, a Captain pilot and a Major pilot who acted as Division Air Officer. The latter served as a coordinator of the flight activities of the

Division. Thus there within the Division were 10 aircraft and 11 pilots. Not always, but often, they all operated from the Division airstrip or base, though frequently each battalion would have a strip near its position, for use during the day and picking up observers for missions. Most of the time, all pilots and crew members were billeted with the Division airstrip, whether at Headquarters Battery, or at the strip itself.

Missions were often assigned to pilots regardless of the battalion to which they belonged, but the primary responsibility of a battalion pilot was to his own battalion. I was the new kid, replacing someone about whom I heard very little. Since I was assigned to Division Artillery Headquarters, I took any kind of mission that came along. I was the only Second Lieutenant, as the others had been overseas as a unit long before I joined them, and had consequently been promoted. Partly due to my having transferred from teaching to flying to overseas as a casual, and partly due to an independence that military training had not entirely suppressed, I was a Second Lieutenant for a long time. A Finance officer once came to New Britain Island from MacArthur's Headquarters, and looked me up while he was there. He said "I have wanted to meet you; you are the highest paid Second Lieutenant in the Pacific." I had some Oregon National Guard duty before the war, and that gave me seniority pay (called a "fogey"), and flight pay which was 50% added to base pay in those days.

We had two L-4s at Division Artillery Headquarters.

The one I flew most was named "Anopheles" for the deadly malaria-carrying mosquito. In other contexts, these airplanes and pilots were dubbed "the mosquito fleet." We sometimes called them "Maytag Messerschmitts." The other L-4 had an interesting name. It was called "Little Bastardo." The reason for this is that the Division had no papers identifying this aircraft nor assigning it to the Division. It had been left behind in the Solomon Islands by a unit preceding the 40th. There appeared to nothing wrong with the airplane. The departing unit must have simply not had room for it. We had a jeep in the same category. I don't know whether its acquisition had been as innocent as that of Little Bastardo.

What we did mostly on New Britain after I arrived was to hold ground and train for our big chance. We were on the southern end of the island, at a place called Cape Gloucester, and the Japanese were on the northern end, at Rabaul. This had been a major base for them, but it was all but neutralized by our steady bombing raids and our by then naval and air superiority. We had outposts at Iboke on the western shore of the southern end, at Talasea, Hoskins, an Australian government outpost about midway on the western shore, and at Arawe, on the eastern shore of the southern end, across from Cape Gloucester. It was at Arawe that The First Marine Division had landed to capture New Britain. We made flights to these places, carrying mail, movie films and personnel. We also performed search missions, trying to spot possible Jap infiltration efforts.

I remember on one trip carrying a Japanese-American soldier who served as an interpreter. We had, at Hoskins, a rare bird: a captured Japanese pilot who, contrary to all of the Japanese propaganda fed to their armed force personnel, was well treated by us, but questioned about their forces. I do not remember whether this was the one who had been a Kamikaze pilot and had bailed out, but we had one such captive. He had had some education in the U. S., and thus spoke some English. He was not convinced of the glory and place in heaven promised to those who gave their lives "willingly" for the Emperor. He had sneaked a parachute aboard on his last flight. A lecture by a Japanese-American scholar of the Kamikaze phenomenon some 50 years later told me that the Kamikaze flights were not all that voluntary, though the pilots were indoctrinated to the point of seeming to be willing to perform the act.

Much of what we did at Cape Gloucester was to train. We practiced short field and road landings; we built air strips in the jungle and flew in and out of them under difficult conditions. We even practiced night flying. We had been given no night flying training. There were no electric systems, and hence no lights on the L-4s. We strapped flashlights on the wing tips and lighted the air strip with Jeep lights. The Artillery General later told us that he didn't want us to fly at night; it was too risky. We were grateful.

I must say something now about that General, Harcourt Hervey. He was a rare National Guard General who was left in command of troops in combat. Most of the original commanders had been replaced by West Point or VMI graduates. General Hervey was not only a good soldier and artilleryman, but a real gentleman. Since he weighed 235 pounds and I weighed 135 pounds, tens of pounds less than any other pilot, the General went with me on these island trips. He would inspect our outposts and bring cheer and lift the morale on these lonely places. We never sent one L-4 alone over the ocean or jungle. The other airplane would carry the mail, movie film, radio communication and maybe a light passenger. The maximum allowed crew weight of the L-4 was 340 pounds. The General and I were over that weight limit without radio or other gear. In all of my more than 50 years of flying, I have never had a more gracious passenger than General Hervey. We shall hear more of him later.

There was an Australian Infantry company at Cape Gloucester, and so we became well acquainted with them, as it was a lonely place. In 1997, I met an Australian who had commanded such a company at Cape Gloucester. Had we met there? We could not tell. There were also some Australian Air Force men and airplanes there, and Australian Army and native government personnel at Hoskins. The Aussies become important later in the story, but for now let me tell about the Aussie pilot who took me up in his fighter plane. It was like our Advanced Trainer AT-6, called the Harvard Trainer by the British. It was manufactured in Australia, called the Whiraway and used as a fighter. He took me through aerobatics to the point where I was completely "wrung out." His turn came to ride in an L-4. You could make an L-4 spin two turns and lose only 400 feet of altitude. This couldn't be done in any other airplane, as far as I know. Over the ocean, I put us into a two-turn spin at 1000 feet. We came out at 600 feet above the water, but he had no idea that this could be done. Then I landed at a strip we had cut out of the jungle half way up the side of a volcano. We landed up hill and took off downhill. It seemed that we were not clearing the trees at the lower end. I did not tell my passenger, but a stream line at the lower end allowed me to turn 45 degrees to the left and go between the trees. My passenger relaxed his grip on the back of my seat and said: "Ow, that's the wy you do it." He said, on landing,: "Matey (pronounced 'Mighty') I think we are even."

American and Australian officers conferring; or were they waiting for the bar to open?

There was also a lonely U. S. Army Air Corps Liaison Pilot left at Cape Gloucester by himself. He nevertheless got a lot of missions to fly; carrying messages and personnel around the island and to New Guinea. He suffered from fatigue, and it was clear from observing him that he should have some rest. One day he passed out at the controls of his L-5. He was fortunate in that he was in straight and level flight, and not headed toward the mountains that are at the center of almost all of those South Sea islands. He came to out of sight of land. He knew the compass heading to land, and luckily he had enough fuel to make it back to land and to his landing strip, which was adjacent to the one we used. He was still there when we shipped out on our next assignment.

Papuans constructing our operations office at Cape Gloucester

Lest you think that all we did at Cape Gloucester was train, train, let me tell you something of our recreational diversions. We had the local Papuans construct us a "grass shack," that we used as a combined office, ready

23

room and recreation center. The mechanics and their helpers lived in squad tents on the airstrip. The pilots lived in tents along with Division artillery headquarters. We all normally ate with Headquarters Battery.

The L-4s came in sturdy wood crates. These were never thrown away. They made good shops, storage sheds and, who knows what? We had one excellent mechanic who had the skills of a moonshiner. He made good raisin brandy, but his corn whiskey was awful. It had not been cured in wooden barrels, which are said to remove the fusel oil, which is what gives you the headaches. The headaches give raw corn whiskey, in the Appalachians, the name "popskull." This sergeant was not from the Appalachians, and did not know about curing whiskey in wooden barrels. He was a Wisconsin grocer.

We had acquired a kerosene-fired refrigerator. Don't ask me where that came from. It was there when I arrived. It was good for our drinks and afternoon snacks, as well as for the occasional party we had in our grass shack.

I can remember the USO-sponsored visits of several Hollywood notables. I remember Jack Benny, Martha Tilton, Carol Landis and Danny Thomas. My apologies to those whom I don't remember. Joe E. Brown, the comic, visited us, but I think that was in the Philippines. It was difficult for him for he had just lost a son to an aircraft accident in one of the services.

We had parties for these who came to Cape Gloucester. They must have been pale things, after the entertainment they received at Division headquarters. Nevertheless, we had steaks, ice cream and other delicacies never ordinarily seen by the troops, or by us, for that matter. How did we get that stuff? Some said that Quartermaster soldiers were corruptible. That is like the john saying that the prostitute is immoral. We corrupted them. We offered airplane rides in exchange for the goodies. Now who is corrupt?

In the same vein as the examples in the previous chapter, it is easy to show that there were many others who had worse times than did we Liaison Pilots. While on a visit to the Australian base of Hoskins, with its grass air strip, we saw an Air Corps twin bomber or attack plane land there with one engine out. I shall not name the airplane. In the first place, I am not sure which one it was. In the second place, the event and its pilot were not complimentary of the airplane, and I don't want to pass judgment on any of those old airplanes. One engine had been shot out; no fault of the airplane or its engine. However, the pilot said that he was very glad to see this grass strip, for the airplane would not hold its altitude on one engine. He had been on a long glide. This was not a good endorsement of the airplane.

Out stepped the pilot, and I said "Hello Frank," and he said "Hello Don." He had been one year behind me in college. He was one of the star football players. While I had been one year in graduate school, he had finished his college work, then entered the service about the same time as I had. We had a nice visit for the rest of the day and the next day. Air Corps personnel appeared the next day, with replacement engine parts and a crew chief to install them. I assume that all went well with the rest of that flight. I had to go on about my business.

The sad part of that story is that I was the last person from home to see Frank. On a later flight, he simply failed to return. He was listed as missing in action. I do not know whether the military ever solved the mystery, but on my return home, Frank's parents had not heard further. He was still officially MIA.

Chapter Four

MABUHAY

It was time to invade the big island of Luzon in the Philippines. Leyte, Samar and Cebu had been taken by the 77th, 7th and Americal Infantry Divisions earlier. We transported the L-4s to the invasion beach by removing the wings, strapping them to the rails on the sides of 2 1/2 ton trucks (the old "6 X 6" GI trucks), and loading the rest of the aircraft aboard the truck. The tail surfaces extended over the cab, with rudder removed, and the propeller was removed so that it would not be damaged by sticking out behind the truck. In this way they were loaded on Navy vessels called "Landing Ships, Tank," or LSTs. The LST was 340 feet long, and quite narrow (I don't remember that dimension). It had no keel, so that it could run aground on the beach. Then the bow would lower, making a ramp on which the cargo of trucks, tanks, jeeps and howitzers could be rolled onto the beach. I do not remember how the deck load of similar equipment got into the hold, to be rolled off of the ship.

We formed a long convoy, which assembled at ports in the Admiralty Islands. Then we headed for Lingayen

Gulf, on the island of Luzon, about 300 kilometers (180 miles) north of Manila. We joined forces with two of the divisions that had captured Leyte and Samar. There were more than 800 ships in our convoy. Kamikaze aircraft attacked repeatedly, but the naval forces leading our armada bore the brunt of the attacks. Two freighters, the John Burke and the Lewis L. Dyche, were blown to bits and sunk. The troop ships were far behind, and we were not aware of the punishment being taken by the Navy.[4] For us, the long and tedious trip to the invasion point was uneventful except for an incident one night. The skipper of our LST was a Lieutenant Senior Grade with little sea experience. The roll of the LST due to its lack of a keel made him seasick. He found that if he were to ride in the wake of the LST ahead of him, he would not get all that nauseating motion. That was fine, except that the convoy made a sharp turn, which caused us to bump the ship ahead. I was glad to be in a lower bunk, for I found myself on the steel deck. I thought we had been torpedoed. No harm had been done, except to the pride of the Skipper and the tranquillity of our sleep.

There was one scene which came back to me recently as one of the follies associated with the war effort. While we were waiting in a harbor in the Admiralty Islands for other ships to join our convoy, I saw something on one of the ships that was puzzling at first. Then I could make it out. Sailors were tossing overboard carcasses of young lamb. In the Army mess, when we were in a stable situation, we sometimes had fresh lamb, which came from Australia, Australian lamb is shipped all over the world and is considered a delicacy in Europe and in the Northeast of the United States. Soldiers didn't like it. They called it "goat" and wouldn't eat it. It is true that Army recipes did not take full advantage of the delicacy of the meat. Lamb stew is not the best you can do with it. Apparently the sailors on that ship wouldn't eat it, either, so overboard it went. The noted anthropologist Margaret Mead characterized the Admiralty Island people as honest and hard working, but very poor. The resources of the islands are not very plentiful; even fishing takes a lot of effort to catch enough for the villages. They would have loved the lamb carcasses. Regulations probably would have prohibited giving them the carcasses, however, Regulations are no doubt silent on tossing "surplus" food overboard.

The forward deck of the LST was crammed with our equipment

On arriving at Lingayen Gulf, we were all deployed in the harbor, waiting our turns at the limited beach space. We filled the harbor, for we were General

29

A small part of the Lingayen Gulf invasion fleet.

Kreuger's 6th Army, consisting of four Infantry divisions. The 40th was a part of the XIV Corps, led by Major General Oscar W. Griswald. Enemy air action had picked up, though it was never in great quantity. We were bombed, however, and some ships were damaged, though ours wasn't. When a raid came, it was my assigned duty to get all army personnel below decks, out of the way of stray bullets and shrapnel. It was a tough job, as no one wanted to be down in that sardine can

A loaded LST waiting it's turn at the invasion beach.

with all the action above. In one raid, I had worked very hard and succeeded. The only personnel on deck were the Navy gunners at their anti-aircraft weapons and me, standing right in the middle of the deck, to see that no soldiers were in sight. A small bomber headed for us, and dropped a bomb. I tried to do what was then expected of me; to get below myself, but my legs would not move. I stood transfixed and paralyzed there while the bomb came down toward us. I would have become only a stain on the deck, except that the bomb wavered and fell harmlessly into the water beside us.

There were other kinds of attack. Small skiffs loaded with explosives were propelled with outboard motors by suicidal Jap boatmen. They wanted to ram the side of your ship, trying to blow a hole in the side of it. Not one of them succeeded, according to S. E. Morison, in "The Liberation of the Philippines".[5] There is more than one way to be a Kamikaze. Mostly, our soldiers with their rifles or carbines shot them. The skiffs became loose floating hazards, and the shooting by our forces posed some hazards to legitimate harbor traffic. There were other attacks, some of which succeeded. They were 18 foot plywood boats, with 260 pounds of explosive and crews of two or three suicide crewmen. One LCI was sunk, while two transports and two LSTs were damaged. The fleet of 70 such craft was decimated the first night that we were in the harbor, however, and gave no trouble, though Kamikaze airplanes continued to attack.[6]

While waiting to beach, our troops were to send an

advance party ashore, to verify the landing site and to lay out space for our deployment beyond the beach. The skipper assigned a not-so-young Lieutenant Junior Grade to escort the party ashore in a small boat. The Lieutenant was what we called "nervous in the service," that is, his combat experience had been so slight that he still showed his fright at being exposed to enemy fire. He dithered and said something like this: "Oh dear, and my wife told me to be careful." We thought this quite funny, but, of course, we were all scared. We later learned to contain it, though it ate our insides every time. One thing that inured you to that fright was being shot at and missed. The bomb scare on the deck at least partially did it for me. I could face enemy fire after that without visible nervousness. I learned that being shot at and hit, if you recovered and returned to battle, had a similar effect. I don't know from experience, for I was never hit.

One thing that our advance parties told us was that the Japs had fled; there were none of them around. On receiving that intelligence and verifying it, Naval units called off the heavy bombardment of the shore and towns of Lingayen and Dagupan. What had been scheduled to be a four hour bombardment was called after a little over two hours. War is a very confused and confusing operation at best, and strange things happen. The intelligence borne by guerrilla forces and our advance party was used to save lives and property. Our forces had warned the Filipino residents to leave the coastal area. It wasn't that simple. Vandalism was a real threat, as it would have been in our society. Therefore they left behind one person for almost every building in the towns. There were injuries; I simply don't remember whether they reported any deaths. The bombardment is a feature of the landing that I had completely forgotten until I read of it in Steinberg's Return to the Philippines.[7] Now I remember vividly the hours of shelling and the appearance of the town as we landed. In those days we didn't have the nice, sanitary term "collateral damage," so we suffered with an old fashioned term like "civilian casualties." It is amazing how glad the residents were to see us, and how friendly they were, in their bombed-out homes. "Mabuhay" is the Filipino greeting. It is like the Hawaiian "Aloha." It means more than "hello." It means "welcome to our islands." We received that greeting many times in the days to follow. It was accompanied by physical evidences of welcome, such as aid to our troops, gifts of food and drink, and simply lots of hospitality.

The wind was not strong, but heavy seas made the beaching rather rough. Our LST battered against the adjacent one, but we made the landing without further incident. On January 10, 1945, 68,000 men were put on shore by nightfall.[8] We rolled the airplanes off the ship. We were assigned a driver and road grader from our Engineer Battalion, and we scratched out an air strip just back from the beach. In two hours, we had one L-4 flying. It went inland along the route taken by the fleeing enemy, to spot and report their position. The airfield at Lingayen was secured the same day, but that was used by Air Force bombers, so we stayed with our grader-made air strips. The Japs offered little resistance, though we were never free of snipers left behind.

I must say here something about the excellent mechanics, or crew chiefs that we had. They kept those L-4s flying and safe in all kinds of conditions. Assembling and checking the first one in two hours is but one example. All ten of the L-4s were flying by the second day. Sergeant Wing was the senior crew chief for Division Artillery, and he kept those men in perfect order and discipline, and the fleet of aircraft ready at all times. Each battalion had one crew chief and one assistant. The assistant did not have the training, but worked with the jeeps and trucks, the fueling and other tasks. We were a smoothly functioning miniature "air armada," and we all had respect for each other and our duties. Other fine men will be recognized later at appropriate times.

There were alternate ways to make assault landings with the L-4s. One unit in I Corps on our left, used an LST in a different way. A plywood "runway" 200 feet long was erected over the forward half of the upper deck. Six L-4s were stacked on their noses; three on either side of this runway. Rudders were removed to clear the space on the runway for a takeoff. One at a time, the L-4s were lifted to the runway. The rudder would be replaced and the engine propped. The LST would head into the wind and gather forward speed. When the air speed was great enough, the pilot would take off. There was no way to return and land on this

200 foot strip of plywood, so the landing had to be made on the beach. All of them made it safely, while we in the 40th Division were unloading and re-attaching the wings to our L-4s. One pilot off of that runway, L. S. "Sam" Sammons, flew up the Tarlac Valley to the San Miguel Brewery. There he landed on a road and duly inquired about any sightings of the fleeing enemy. Someone came out from the brewery and presented him with cases of beer. There were cordial mabuhays all around. Sammons then landed on our air strip and was with us for a few days.

Our objectives were, along with other elements of XIV Corps and General Swift's I Corps on our left, to clear the Tarlac Valley. We were to follow the Tarlac river upstream and then take back Clark Field, a major air base, Ft. Stotsenberg, and Camp O'Donnell. Camp O'Donnell is where the Americans captured at Corregidor were housed. By the time we arrived there, all of the prisoners had been transferred to Bilibid prison, near Manila. All of these objectives were about half way from the Gulf to Manila. There was not much resistance in our sector, on the right side of the Valley, but I Corps, on the left met a lot of resistance. Sleeping at night was hazardous, as raiding parties would descend on us. We would sleep on the ground wherever the day's advance placed us at dark. Sleeping with the 45 caliber pistol under our makeshift pillow became a habit. We would build a new air strip almost every day. The Engineer with the road grader stayed with us, and Headquarters provided a guard detail.

An L-4 departing from a 200 foot plywood deck on an LST.

Chapter Five

CLARK FIELD
OR BUST

The entire 6th Army, including us, General Rapp Brush's 40th Infantry Division, moved up the Tarlac Valley. We, along with the 37th Division, were the XIV Corps. We traveled on the main highway in trucks, or as foot soldiers in routes parallel to the highway. The air section leapfrogged the Artillery, sending part of our ground crew forward with the Engineer and road grader, to scrape out a new strip for us. We would fly to it for the night's lodging (actually, sleeping on the ground), and the next day's flying. Small enemy raids attacked us a few times at night. There were several occasions when we were strafed from the air. There was nothing we could do about that, but some of the trucks in the main convoy had machine guns mounted on them, and they gave a good account of themselves. I do not recall their downing any of the airplanes, but they worried the Jap pilots. There were not many Jap airplanes or pilots left, so that our Luzon campaign was relatively free of air attacks.

Meeting little resistance, we were frequently running off our battle maps. Early in the century, when Douglas MacArthur was still a Captain, he headed a team that mapped the Philippines. They were excellent battle maps, of a scale 1 to 50,000, showing great detail of terrain. They had been updated to show cities, towns and installations. At one point The Air Officer sent me back down the river to Lingayen to get a load of maps needed for planning the next day's advance and potential battles. They decided not to wait for a delivery by truck, which would not have arrived until the next day. They wanted to plan that night. I loaded the back seat and cargo deck with maps and started back up the river.

What a dull damned flight! I decided to practice my precision contour flying, by staying in the river bed, keeping my right wing tip a constant distance from the treetops. Around a bend I met a DC-3 (military C-47). He was doing roughly the same thing. Luckily, our training paid off when we needed it. On meeting anything head on, a pilot's reaction is supposed to be a hard right turn. We both did it. The main wheels of a C-47 retract into wells, but there is no cover. I remember seeing the grooves on his tires as they went past my left window. I do not know what he carried, but a little later C-47s carried wounded soldiers from a M.A.S.H. hospital back to a base hospital in Tacloben, on Leyte Island. Wounded soldiers and maps would have been strewn all over that river bed, but for our conditioned reflexes.

Division Headquarters eagerly took the maps I

brought, leaving only one set for the air strip. Early the next morning, the Air Officer selected me to fly to the target area and adjust artillery fire on a base point and two check points. They call this "registration," and it is done prior to an expected battle. It creates the possibility of the accurate shifting of fire short distances from one of these points. They thus waste no time in zeroing in on a real enemy target. One section of the map set we had was relevant, and, remember, we had only one set. Another pilot, a Lieutenant Lynn Fuller, was in the back seat as observer. The Cub has a folding door for access on the right side. The top half, made of Plexiglas, folds up against the underside of the right wing. In the tropics, we took that off and stored it, using only the lower, fabric covered, half of the door. This meant that we always had a good breeze going on the right side. Thus if anything was to go from front to back or vice versa, one had to pass it over the left shoulder of the pilot.

Dumb me, I tried to pass the map to Lynn over my right shoulder. You guessed it; it fluttered down into the rice paddies, while the fire direction center was counting on us to do their registrations. When does the court martial begin? We watched it flutter down, but lost sight of it before it hit ground. Rice paddies typically had dikes of about one foot width separating them. There was, however, below us, a single track straight road between paddies. I gave it a low drag to see whether my main landing gear wheels would fit on the road, as their span was a little wider than a truck's. They would fit.

There were telephone poles along the side, but I could fit my 36 foot wing span in with a foot or two to spare. We landed, but could not see the map. I taxied to the intersection of this road with the main road. A battalion of Infantry (ours) came along, headed for the front. I spotted the Lt. Colonel leading the column, went up to him, saluted and said something like: "Sir have you seen a map that fell from my airplane?" He assumed a tired look that said "Now I think I have seen everything" and replied: "No lieutenant, I haven't seen your map."

Lynn turned the airplane around (It has a hand grip near the tail, and is a light lift with no one aboard.) Since there was no wind, we took off in the direction from which we had come. As we got off the ground, we saw a soldier running across the dry paddies waving our map. It was one of our Artillerymen, who was laying telephone wire up to the front. We landed again. "Hey Lieutenant, you dropped something," the Artilleryman said. I swear that he actually used that cliché. We retrieved the map and took off again. We flew to the target area and checked in with the fire direction center. They were not quite ready for us. Therefore, they had not missed us at all. This story was not told until much later.

We continued past the town of Tarlac to a village called Bamban, where we had to wait for the action to catch up with us. This was near the northern edge of Clark Field, which the Japs were vigorously defending. We scraped out a landing strip on the edge of the village, and commandeered a peasant house for our office and

40

Looking across rice paddies and Bamban to Clark Field.

Bamban was nearly destroyed by the fighting.

41

sleeping quarters for the pilots. The mechanics set up tents for their quarters. We constructed a shower of an old fuel drum mounted on a scaffold, with the tropical sun to heat the water, with duck boards (a wooden grill on which to stand, allowing water to flow away beneath them) and a burlap curtain for privacy. Real living!

The owner of the house would come around every three or four days, and inquire as to when he could have his house back. Our Division Air Officer, a very congenial Major named Jim Williams, would reply with the Filipino equivalent of "manana." Several times, Major Jim would ask the house owner what were those digging disturbances in the yard. The reply would be a finger to the lips and a shake of the head. Finally, just about the time that he could have his house back manana, actually meaning tomorrow, he told us that those diggings were the graves of Jap soldiers. You have perhaps inferred from the shower that peasant houses have no bathroom. So, we dug the familiar G. I. latrine, complete with bench seat and tarp screen. When we departed, we left behind a digging disturbance similar to those we had questioned. Was the house owner pulling our legs? Were those digs simply covered up latrines? We'll never know. We had dug ourselves fox holes in the yard, and we filled them in when we left. There were so many fresh diggings in this family's yard that it looked like a graveyard without head stones. More of Bamban later, as we spent a long time there.

Chapter Six

MARIO

This chapter reports one-on-one combat, with a hint of cannibalism, so those with delicate stomachs might want to skip it.

The way in which the Filipinos eagerly greeted us and did everything they could to help us was impressive and gratifying. You would see a column of Infantrymen marching toward the front and a ragged column of Filipino boys alongside carrying the soldiers' packs. Many of these young men had older brothers, fathers or uncles who served as guerrilla soldiers, with various weapons and tactics, awaiting our arrival. You will hear more of them later. These younger boys wanted to get into the act, and they did.

While we were moving up the Tarlac Valley, creating a new airstrip every day or two, Mario, a young man from a village, attached himself to us. He was a remarkably bright and able young man. He could prepare food like a pro. We were supplied with "C" rations, consisting of four or five varieties of canned meat dishes and some hard biscuits. They were horrible if eaten cold. We did have coffee, and there was a lemonade powder that we must have mishandled because its taste led us to call it "battery acid." Maybe we should have had some sugar. We were provided a gasoline-fired field range, with which we heated our cans of C rations, made coffee and heated water for sponge baths and shaving. Our discipline required us to shave every day, regardless of combat conditions. Mario could do wonders with these C rations, with local flavoring and herbs. We would send him into a village with money and/or cigarettes, and he would return with chickens, eggs, fruits, vegetables and wine. He prepared great dishes for us. We were really living!

Mario had a hobby. In a cage he had what we at first called a "rooster." In no way was it a rooster. It was a fighting cock. Cock fighting was a great sport in the Philippines. Mario would coach and train this bird to lunge, by thrusting his fist into the bird's face. He would groom this creature and spit-polish his gleaming red and yellow neck feathers. The bird stood tall and proud, strutting around. We thought he looked like General MacArthur. We called him "MacArthur."

One evening, before we had our meal, some boys came out from a near-by village. They had a fighting cock. He was a scruffy, mean-looking bird. He had scars from earlier fights. Handlers attached razor-sharp, curved spurs of about four inches in length to the feet of these birds for the fights. There was usually only one survivor, and maybe none. We thought this bird must be a mean fighter. We called him "Tojo." Of course, these boys challenged Mario. MacArthur had not yet been in a fight, and Mario was not sure that he was ready. With goading by the village boys and encouragement by us, he finally accepted the challenge. We made a ring; and prepared seating on Jerry cans, logs or crates. Bets were laid and the small crowd, supplemented by a few more boys from the village, was assembled. The handlers attached the spurs to the birds' legs and held them firmly while they pecked each other on the head to get the adrenaline flowing.

Then they released the birds in the ring. They circled, feinted and stuck their necks out at each other. Then Tojo lowered his head and charged. Alas! MacArthur fled. He went out through the crowd and into the boondocks, as people dodged those fearsome spurs on his feet. (Boondocks is a Filipino word, meaning the same thing there as it does in America: "the boonies.") The boys from the village were peasants, while Mario was very much middle class. They enjoyed taunting Mario in his extreme humiliation. He was crushed. We did not know what they were saying to him amid all that laughter, but those local languages sounded raunchy, with their repeated syllables. Mario captured MacArthur, took off his spurs and threw him into the cage. He then went into the supply tent, to the cot we had given him. We ate cold C rations that night.

Mario was up bright and early the next morning, however. We could hear him firing up the gasoline range, putting on our coffee and heating our shaving water. We filled our steel helmets with water, and went about our morning splashing and shaving. We could smell the coffee, and we heard a strange frying noise. Then we smelled it. Fried chicken for breakfast! There was a piece for each of us. As we bit into it, someone asked: 'Mario, where did you get the chi---?' Then we saw the empty cage. "Poor MacArthur!"

Mario left us when we were established for a long stay in Bamban. We didn't need him any longer, as we took our meals with the Headquarters Battery of Division Artillery.

Chapter Seven

LOOK JULIUS,
NO BULLET HOLES

B efore we reached Bamban north of Clark Field and Ft. Stotsenberg, we located ourselves near Camp O'Donnell, from which the American prisoners had been transferred to the Bilibid prison. I did not witness the rescue, nor did I see any of the prisoners. I have seen pictures of them many times, however. The human body resists death by starvation by eating itself as long as there is strength left. These men were as close to the proverbial "skin and bones" as any I have ever seen pictured. The starvation began on the march from Corregidor to O'Donnell. It is reported that any who dropped by the trail's side were shot by their Jap guards. It is stories like these that made our attacks on the enemy easy on our consciences.

A Lieutenant from Division Artillery Intelligence, Julius Leetham, came down with a mission, and the Major selected me to fly him. He had a big bundle of leaflets, printed in Japanese, calling on the enemy to surrender, as his position was hopeless. I have no record of any Jap surrendering because of one of these pamphlets. In any case, headquarters did not know the locations of those who had fled Clark Field and Ft. Stotsenberg. We were to find them and drop our little message on them. Anywhere where we saw more than one enemy, or at any well-used trail intersection, we were to drop them. We were both skeptical of this mission, but like good soldiers, set off on it. After what seemed futile pamphlet dropping around Camp O'Donnell, we went into the Zambales Mountains, west of Clark Field.

All at once, we saw a massing of troops and equipment below us, and a great deal of activity. Some of the activity was aiming various weapons at us. I said something stupid, like: "Judd, throw out the rest of those dumb pamphlets, I'm going to show you a maneuver called 'getting the hell out of here'." I immediately flew down to within feet of the ground, and over a ridge into the next valley. It was fully occupied, too. All soldiers appeared to be in foxholes or caves. I reduced the standard 800 feet of elevation above the ground to not much more than 8 feet. I flew down the ridges and valleys, toward Clark Field and the Tarlac valley.

Going over another ridge resulted in no improvement, for the next valley seemed to be just as fully occupied as the last one. I kept low, so that they could not have shot at the airplane silhouette against the sky. To do this, where there were tree lines, I tried not to go over them, but to go into a nearly 90 degree bank, to go between trees. I also stayed low so that these troops in foxholes and caves could not see me coming, though they could hear me. My thought was, that if they could get a straight head-on shot, they would probably have hit us, or if they had a silhouette against the sky, they had a good chance at a hit. I made sure to give them only a view of my tail as I sped away. It was not that we were going faster than their bullets, but by the time the rifle bullets reached what they were aiming at, we were no longer there. A rifle bullet does not travel in a perfectly flat trajectory; there is a slight sag in it. On a firing range with fixed targets, you set the sights for range. They had no way to do that, nor to lead me in their aiming. By maintaining complete surprise, I gave them no chance to set up machine guns, whose tracer bullets would have aided them in finding the range. Of course, they had no time in which to set up their 70 mm. anti-aircraft weapons, which they certainly had.

Julius was pessimistic, and I suppose we believed the propaganda that they would torture and kill us if we survived a crash in their area, just as they believed that we would do the same. Julius took his 45 caliber pistol from its holster and said something dumb, like: "I have six bullets for these bastards and two for us." That was much too pessimistic, for I had confidence in my crop duster flying skills.

It seemed like a long time. We had no time to look at watches nor at air speed. However, looking at the distance on the map afterward, and guessing that we were going 85 to 90 mph, we had to conclude that the shooting could not have lasted more than five or six minutes. The L-4's cruising speed was 70 mph, but we were going down slope at full throttle. The Japs nevertheless fired hundreds of rounds at us, but all were from behind us. It was remarkable, still, that there were no bullet holes in the airplane when we landed, though there were weeds on our landing gear. The absence of bullet holes so impressed Julius that he said: "I now have so much confidence in you that I would fly with you through a brick wall." I never asked him to do that. There was a standard issue of brandy; an Air Corps custom of giving air crews a shot after a grueling mission. This is the only time that I asked for such a shot. Otherwise, we kept the brandy for parties.

The sequel to this story came along immediately after the flight. One of our missions was to find and report the positions of the enemy. Accordingly, we went to Division Artillery headquarters and made our report. A staff person was busily putting pins in their situation map to correspond with our report. Either XIV Corps or 6th Army was coming for a visit, which always meant an inspection, as Army veterans will recall. A Colonel in headquarters was "nervous in the service" about this visit; as they came in, he said something like: "Get these people out of here." So we left. Julius was a member of that headquarters, so I assume that he went back and helped them complete putting pins in the situation map. My memory is not that good, but I have a faint recollection that someone put us in for medals as a result of that flight. Nothing came of it, if someone indeed had recommended us. Headquarters wasn't that impressed.

What we had seen was not trivial. I have learned recently that units of the 40th Division captured one area in those mountains that was 300 yards by 75 yards, containing one 70 mm. field piece, 17 light machine guns, 150 rifle pits or foxholes and three 90 mm. Mortars.[9] This was the kind of concentration of weapons that appeared to be where we were flying that day.

Chapter Eight

MED EVAC
AND ACK ACK

W hile we were operating out of our little air strip at Bamban, a young Air Corps Staff Sergeant who was a Liaison Pilot, would sometimes stay with us. He was attached to a nearby hospital, a M.A.S.H., or military auxiliary surgical hospital. Its more familiar format is the M*A*S*H of the television show of the same name. The mission was the same as in the TV show; emergency treatment of battle wounded, and preparation of them for movement to a base hospital for long-term care. With Alan Alda, Loretta Switt and Jamie Farr, however, you heard the chop-chop of the helicopters bringing the "fresh meat." Believe it or not, in WWII, we did not have helicopters. Most of the patients were brought in by ambulance. This young pilot, however, flew one of the L-5s with the side opening for a stretcher patient. He flew all day, bringing in patients from south of where we were, on the route to Manila.

He liked to stay with us sometimes, for we had

excellent mechanics to check his L-5, while he had none at the hospital. He was entirely on his own, as far as the L-5 was concerned. There was an air strip bigger than ours, from which C-47s flew, transporting patients to a base hospital in Tacloban. All of their fueling and servicing was done at the other end, so there were no services at the hospital end. He was perfectly welcome to share our facilities.

One evening the Sergeant asked us whether we had noticed that the paint job on his wings did not match that on the fuselage. Someone replied that he had assumed that they were replacements for original wings, but he was curious about the story of the wings. The Sergeant replied that one day, after picking up a litter patient near Manila, he received enemy anti-aircraft fire. They were bursting shells, or ack-ack. One burst so closely that it tore off a large section of his right wing tip. This made it difficult to hold his course. He could not avoid making wide turns to the right. He could make a little progress north toward the hospital on each turn, but there was the question of whether his fuel would hold out for such slow progress north. There was the immediately more uncomfortable fact that they would still fire at him while he was on the southern parts of his loops.

Then it happened. He was hit again. This time, the bursting shell tore off a great chunk of his left wing tip. He could then straighten up and fly north. Progress was still slow, for it took full throttle to simply maintain altitude, and the necessary high angle of attack eliminated any hope of much air speed above the stalling speed. However, he did make it back to the hospital.

Back at the base there was a damaged L-5 with wings still intact. On the next empty C-47 coming to the M*A*S*H, they brought him two wings and a mechanic to install them. His old wings still graced a trash dump behind the hospital. That was his story, and he stuck to it. Who were we to question the Sergeant?

Chapter Nine

TIPS AND
TANKS

While we were at Bamban, trying to take Clark Field, we were visited by an Artillery Liaison Pilot from one of the units that had landed on the Bataan Peninsula. The XI Corps was the force, including the 38th Infantry Division and the 34th Combat Team.[10] I am not sure to which of these units the pilot belonged. They had landed on the western shore of the Bataan Peninsula, and were to join forces with us. The Lieutenant had flown a senior officer up to confer with our leadership. He stayed with us at the airstrip while the senior officer had other accommodations.

After the day's work, we would gather for evening relaxation. To help us relax, we bought local wine. Some of the five gallon Jerry cans that we had were porcelain-lined, with a spigot on the bottom of each of them. They were designed to hold water, milk, fruit juice and the like. Wine was not on the approved list, but who counted? We would get the five gallons of wine in a village shop, put the can on a table or stump, and be ready for what we would now call a virtual evening campfire. Of course, we could not have a fire, or even a light. So we would tell our stories in complete darkness. In the tropics there is not much twilight, so it gets dark quickly after an early sunset.

The Lieutenant told us of an earlier flight he had made soon after landing on Bataan. His Commanding Officer sent him over the mountains to see what he could see. He reached a valley or plain, which extended from Subic Bay down toward Manila, and lay between his forces and ours. On that plain, he saw what appeared to be a platoon of Japanese Infantry. He flew over to look, and found that he was right. So, of course, they fired rifles at him. His airplane was hit. They knocked off one tip of his propeller. When this much unbalance happens to a propeller, the vibration immediately becomes so severe that the engine must be shut down, or it will tear itself off of its mounts. So, he had to land in a field. It was the dry season, so the field (probably a rice paddy) was firm. The problem was that the Japs were coming after him. He was, to say the least, concerned. We carried, as a seat cushion, a pack that contained emergency food, disinfectant, water purification tablets, bandages and a folding machete. He took out the machete and hacked off the other propeller tip. There is a brass ferule on the leading edge of the wooden propeller that he could not cut, but it was sticking out on the bullet-shattered tip, too. So he had a pretty ragged propeller.

It worked. He could get off in the space available,

and he eluded the foot soldiers. The engine had to be revved up to provide enough thrust, and the vibration was still pretty great. He was able to fly far enough to escape the enemy infantry, but the vibration eventually split a seam in the fuel tank. The L-4 has one twelve gallon tank in the fuselage, riding right over the knees of the pilot. All of the remaining fuel came down over his knees and feet. Of course, he had to land again. This time he was near a village, and the enemy apparently did not see him.

Some young men came out from the village, asking whether they could help. Indeed they could. The Lieutenant wrote out a message, giving the map coordinates of his position, and asking for a propeller, a fuel tank and five gallons of gasoline. He asked a young man to take it to his unit, roughly describing where that could be found. You see, he had to trust the local people. His trust was well advised. The young man departed at once. A guard of young men was placed on the airplane. In the village he was wined and dined. He was given quarters for the night, and provided with a peasant girl for the night.

Some of the listeners at first held the view that Filipinos must be immoral people, because of the peasant girl aspect of the story. We had to remember that the Filipino population of that time lived, certainly in the country side, in a feudal society. In such a society, middle class and upper class girls are very carefully chaperoned. With peasant girls, the opposite is true. They may be articles of commerce or party favors, with little embarrassment to the girls or to their families. Each class of the society was true to its own moral code. There was nothing unusual in the entertainment that he had received. It was simply an indication that the Filipino people were very loyal to us, and helpful whenever they could do something for us.

The rest of the story is that the young messenger must have traveled all night, for by noon the next day, another L-4 arrived with the requested material, plus a mechanic. That L-4 was heavily loaded. The empty fuel tank rode on the knees of the mechanic, and the propeller was over his shoulder. Where were the five gallon Jerry can of fuel and the tool box? Who knows? Anyway, the repairs were soon made and both L-4s were off to rejoin their unit. All that the villagers had was a set of battered souvenirs and the possibility of a pregnant peasant girl.

The days were sometimes nerve wracking, and we used the wine to "wind down," we thought, in order to fall asleep and get a restful night. We may have overdone it some evenings. Modern medical research has come up with the finding that alcohol-induced sleep is not sound, nor particularly restful. The wine may make the imbiber hard to arouse, but this does not mean that he or she is in a restful sleep. Even if we had known all of that, we probably would have drunk the wine anyway.

There is a sequel to our wine drinking evenings. Years later, while residing in Michigan and being on the faculty of Michigan State University, I was getting

Army Reserve training. The Department of Defense (DOD) paid the rent on civilian airplanes in which I got the flying part of my training. Eighty hours a year were necessary for me to keep my Liaison Pilot rating. One of our veteran pilots from the 40th Division lived in Peoria, Illinois and arranged a small reunion. The DOD would let me get a certain portion of my time in a complex aircraft, that is, one with constant speed propeller and retractable landing gear. On this occasion I rented a Bonanza and invited my Reserve Artillery Battalion Commander to go with me. We enjoyed a good mini-vacation in Peoria, flying down from Lansing, Michigan.

There was a young man at the reunion, from Chicago, I think. He had been a Sergeant in the 40th Division Artillery. He had been the sergeant in charge of the security guard at the airstrip one night when the strip was raided by a Jap patrol. Shots were flying all around. He tried to wake the pilots. They should have been in their foxholes, at the least. At best, he might expect some help from them. They all had 45 caliber pistols, after all. He was very angry with the pilots that night. They had drunk so much wine that they could not be wakened by all that firing, nor by his shouts. We were not always as alert or as helpful as we could have been.

Chapter Ten

DOUGOUT DOUG

Rapid movement toward Manila and prompt capture of Clark Field were important objectives for General MacArthur. He had ordered the dropping of match books and candy bars containing the slogan: "I shall return" for several months before the invasions of which we were a part. We had a little irritation at the "I" part of it, because, remember, there were 68,000 of us in that one landing alone. We had no doubts about his courage or about his skill. It was his ego that bothered us. Also, and I hope to find out someday, whether the rumors about his home that Engineers built for him at Hollandia in New Guinea were true, or exaggerations. The story was that it was a mansion. I suspect now that the stories were exaggerations. I know two veteran Army Engineers who were at Hollandia. Neither remembers seeing the home, though they agree that it was built. We know that his family was with him. By the time we were supposed to have captured Clark Field, many of the men I worked with had been overseas for forty months, with no break. I had been over less than a year, so I did not feel that aspect of it quite so keenly.

On January 25th we heard over the news broadcast from the United States that we, the 40th Division, had captured Clark Field as a birthday present for General MacArthur. His 65th birthday was the next day. Remember, we had been on Luzon only for 15 days, and we felt that we had traveled a long way in that time. We laughed uproariously at the notion that we had captured Clark Field. We were there, but it was still "hot."

Our Division Air Officer, Major Jim Williams, knew very well two Captains who were with Air Corps Intelligence. Their mission was to get to captured and abandoned enemy materiel and to get samples of it for further study. They felt that they had to get to their prizes before the foot soldiers got there, for the soldiers were avid souvenir hunters. So, these two intrepid Captains, with two Jeeps and drivers, were frequently out front where they should not have been, according to prudent practice for the rest of us.

On the morning of January 26, Jim was flying gingerly over Clark field, half expecting to be shot at. There he saw two U. S. Jeeps creeping along. He throttled back so that his voice could be heard, glided down almost to the level of the Jeeps, and shouted: "Hey, you damned fool, you'll get your ass shot off!" Then the corncob pipe and the cap with all the gold scrambled eggs peeked out from one of the Jeeps. It was Dugout Doug MacArthur himself.

64

Jim told us about this at lunch time. He then asked: "How much trouble do you think I'm in?" (Each aircraft had its unique numbers a foot high on the side of the fuselage and two feet high under one wing.) We thought about it a minute, and concluded: "You are in no trouble at all: MacArthur loved it." I am still looking for a reference to that incident in something MacArthur may have written. In his "Reminiscences" MacArthur mentions the fact that his staff people complained that he took too many chances. There was no mention of our Major's rude remarks to him, however.

The announcement about the birthday present had either come from MacArthur's headquarters, or at the least his headquarters had approved it. The General apparently was a man who believed his own propaganda. One who believes his own propaganda is either a hero or a dangerous man. We recognized Mac Arthur as a skilled General and a hero to many people, regardless of our irritation at his ego. He certainly was a hero of the war in the Pacific, and he was a hero in his rehabilitation of Japan. Remember, he had every bit as much reason as any of us had to resent what the Japanese had done in the Pacific, and the vicious way in which they resisted us. He became a revered leader to the Japanese, as he had been to the Filipinos.

However, he became a dangerous man when he wanted to follow the Chinese army across the Yalu River and to fight them on their own soil during the Korean War. President Truman had the sense to know when he became dangerous and the courage to say "Enough."

Chapter Eleven

SO SORRY, NO AMMO

I wish that I could claim to have discovered this target, but I cannot. Our Air Officer went to Division Headquarters where they were studying aerial photos of the area. This structure, though well camouflaged, looked suspicious in the photos, and not quite like the hill that I had thought it to be. Major Williams, with captain Robert Munyon, Aide to General Brush, then flew a low reconnaissance. It was at Fort Stotsenberg, about two miles from Clark Field, toward the mountains. Division Headquarters thought it to be either an ammunition dump or an equipment storage building.

At any rate, they called for Naval bombardment, thinking that this was more than an appropriate artillery target. I was asked whether I knew the site. I did. I had not yet decided whether it was something on which I should call in artillery fire. The air Officer asked me to circle over it, beginning fifteen minutes before the scheduled arrival of Naval bombers.

The Naval planes carried several bombs. I circled at a little more than the proverbial 800 feet, to give them plenty of room to get under me. When the target was hit, it began to explode, in repeated bursts. The Navy gave it several bomb runs. It was getting to be dangerous to be near it. It was indeed an ammunition dump. It burned and exploded for three days. The Navy must have liked this target, for the bombers came back the second day and stimulated the burning and exploding with several more bombing passes.

The destruction of this ammunition dump explains some of our good fortune in days to follow. The Japs were low on ammunition. They had dual purpose anti-aircraft artillery, with which they could fire at us in the air or on the ground. They occasionally did both, though in a very limited manner. They would fire rounds which we interpreted to be adjusting rounds, getting the range and deflection correct. In the air, we would see one round behind us, and then one in front of us, or vice versa. That would be the signal to take evasive action. Dutch Schultz, in his wonderful book, Janey[11] indicated that he would go into a spin in such a situation. Why didn't I think of that at this time? If the Allied forces had been firing at a target such as I presented in the air, we would then fire a volley of rounds halfway between our "short" and our "over" rounds. In this case nothing happened. The Jap was through firing; he probably had used his ammunition allotment for the morning. My evasive actions were not spins, but strange flying. I would kick rudder, sending us skidding all over the sky, and I would do other things to make the path of the L-4 unpredictable. About half the time I would have an observer in the rear seat. This was very uncomfortable for him. He could not wear his steel helmet, for he had to use ear phones. I would tell him to bring it along for reasons he would later understand. It was far better for the observers to fill their helmets with their breakfast than to get a bullet hole. I never did get a bullet hole in an airplane I was flying, as pilot or passenger. Some airplanes that I flew had bullet holes in them, but they had been acquired by someone else.

The same desultory firing pattern prevailed when the dual purpose artillery was aimed at us on the ground. An "over" and a "short" would prompt us to cower in our foxholes, but nothing would happen. Eventually, we came to ignore the firing; but we might have been sadly awakened one day had the Jap really begun to fire the artillery seriously. It didn't happen. We liked to credit this good fortune to the Navy's destruction of the ammunition dump, due in large measure to our detection and call for Naval bombing.

Chapter Twelve

FLIES, MINES
AND MARKED MAPS

S anitary conditions may not have been top flight in the Philippines before the war. Whatever they were, they had deteriorated because of the war and occupation conditions. Flies and mosquitoes were everywhere. We had some protections against mosquitoes. We slept under nets every night, when the mosquitoes were most evident. We also took Atabrine, a substitute for the quinine that had been the universal preventive before the Japanese captured the sources of the drug. We believed that Atabrine warded off the disease. Later information tells us that it suppressed the symptoms, but did not prevent the virus from being in our system. In any case, I personally do not know for sure that I had any symptoms after returning home and stopping the medication. I do know of one officer who was lax in his dosage of Atabrine, and suffered Malaria symptoms both before and after returning home.

Flies were a much worse menace. They were everywhere, and on everything. The local population suffered greatly from baccilary dysentery. It was especially disastrous for infants. They would become dehydrated and die. One of the saddest sights in the villages was the frequent funeral processions with the tiny coffins.

I contracted baccilary dysentery, which was a serious matter. They did not hospitalize me, but kept me in a "sick bay" type of tent for five days. At the end of that time, I was returned to "light duty." We did not know what was light duty for a pilot. We finally decided that I should not actually fly an airplane, but that it was all right for me to go as an observer.

Lieutenant Fisher had a mission and asked me to go along as an observer. We finished our mission and descended from the mountains, over Clark Field. It was securely in our hands by then. The problem with it was that we had the correct information that the Japs had planted land mines. We did not think that our Engineers had yet had time to clear the mines. The hour or so of flight and subsequent descent in altitude combined to put me in misery. I told Lieutenant Fisher that he had a difficult choice to make: If he wanted a clean airplane, we must land at once. We were not close enough to our strip in Bamban. We did not use a runway; that would be too obvious a place for a land mine. The taxi ways were not paved, so that we could see whether the soil had been disturbed, by flying low and slow along them. Lt. Fisher chose a pristine taxi way for an uneventful landing and everything was right with the world for the flight back to Bamban.

Lieutenant Fisher soon found an opportunity to transfer to the First Cavalry Division. He was not one of the original Guardsmen (few of us pilots were), and chose the greater glamour of the "First Cav." I was transferred to the 143rd Field Artillery Battalion, to take his place. On my first day with them, I discovered the Commander, Lieutenant Colonel Wallace Nickell's practice of having dinner with his officers, combat conditions or not. I sneaked in and sat at the foot of the table, as seemed appropriate for a new kid, who was still a Second Lieutenant. Col.Nickell asked me: "Moore, are you First or Second?" I knew that he meant in rank, and not in any other order of things. I replied: "Second, Sir." He turned to his Adjutant and said: "Bromley, get on that." I was a First Lieutenant the next week.

Lt. Colonel Nickell is another of the fine officers who should be commended here. He was one of the old National Guardsmen who had been President of an oil company in civilian life. He sounded gruff and short, but he had every consideration for his officers and men. He knew what he was doing, expected us to know as much, and was not loath to give us credit for what we knew and did. The 40th was called out again in the Korean War, and Col. Nickell became the Artillery General. They could not have made a better choice.

My new companion pilot was Fred Kutisch. I flew the airplane that Lt. Fisher had left behind. It had no name, and I didn't attempt to give it one. I was flying it on a mission one day, with Fred Kutisch as my observer. We were flying over enemy territory when I attempted to

73

pass the map back to Fred. Remember the missing door and the necessity of passing over the left shoulder? Well, I forgot. The map went out, floating down toward the enemy. We had plenty of maps, but there is a regulation against letting any map with markings on it fall into enemy hands. Again, when does the court martial begin?

Fred said: "Cut it up with your propeller." That was as good an idea as any. I dived at it and missed. It floated down slowly, and we still had enough altitude. I dived again. It seemed as if I would have to make a slight right turn in order to hit it with my propeller. Instead, I had an inspiration, and kicked hard left rudder. The L-4 skidded to the right, in the direction of the map. I raised my right wing slightly, and the map slid along the underside of the wing, bounded past the wing strut, and into the cabin. We went back to Bamban as if nothing had happened. We did not tell that story until much later. I thought that maybe the statute of limitations had expired. I don't know how many pilots believed the story, but it was my story and I stuck to it. Fred was my witness.

The crew chief for the 143rd Battalion was Sergeant Johnson. His first name has faded from my memory. I always addressed him as "Sergeant Johnson," trying not to become familiar. He was an excellent mechanic and soldier. The airplanes of the 143rd were always in as good condition as could be managed, given their age and rough use.

Chapter Thirteen

GOODBYE JIM AND LITTLE BASTARDO

In any Army unit, in war or in peace, there are the good guys and the not-so-good guys. It was no different in the 40th Division Artillery, or "Divarty," as we called it. I did not know many people apart from Artillery, so I can write only about Artillerymen and local people like Mario. Most of the Filipinos I knew were fine people, too. Shall I write about the not-so-good guys? I do not know yet.

I have told you about General Hervey, the Artillery General. He was a great friend and leader. I will tell you more of him as appropriate.

One of the best was Major Jim Williams, the Division Air Officer, who was in a staff position, not a command position. He was responsible for coordinating all air operations and the operation of the air strip or airstrips. Except for the two other pilots in Divarty, we were all responsible to Artillery battalion commanders. While I was still in Divarty headquarters, I worked closely with Jim.

Jim was a Los Angeles business man and National Guard Infantry officer. He was interested enough in flying to apply for and receive the Liaison Pilot training and the tactical flying training at the Artillery School. He and the others of the original Guardsmen had been in the Pacific area for forty months at the time we first arrived at Clark Field.

General Rapp Brush awards the Air Medal to his Aide, Captain Bob Mumyan Division Air Officer Major Jim Williams is at the left.

A friend of Jim's, the Aide to General Brush, Captain Bob Munyon, flew with Jim frequently. Jim was definitely not "nervous in the service." He flew dangerously close to enemy positions. On one mission, Jim and Bob came back with 120 bullet holes in the airplane, "Little Bastardo."   Bob later recalls that was probably double counting, as 60 bullets must have gone in one side and come out the other, or gone through the bottom of a wing and out the top.

Later a Major Frank Ribbel came to the strip from the Judge Advocate General section. He reported to Major Jim that the Infantry unit to which both Majors had once belonged was pinned down near Fort Stotsenberg. They both wanted to do something about it. We really had to learn that there was not much that we could do in most cases like that. We always wanted to try, nonetheless.

Jim and his friend took off while I was flying a mission. I heard some confused transmissions over the Artillery net. Jim said something like: "My observer is hit."   After that, the transmissions became garbled. I strongly suspected that Jim was hit, too. He started using the call sign of Anopheles, the airplane I was flying. Actually, they were in Little Bastardo, the other Divarty airplane. When I returned to the air strip, I was greeted with an ambulance and a concerned group of people. When they saw that I was all right, they were almost angry with me. We immediately became concerned for the two Majors, and we soon learned the worst. They had crashed and burned. They had gotten too close, and had been gunned down.

All of the pilots were at the funeral, except for one who was on a necessary mission. Most of the ground crew was there, too. General Hervey gave the eulogy at Jim's funeral, and cried. Many of the old Guardsmen were his friends, and he felt that way about them.

General Hervey took the pilots aside after the ceremony. He told us that he did not want us to become brave like Jim had. He said that he wanted us alive. We cooled it, at least for a while. His words did have an effect on our decisions as to where and how to fly. Some of us may be here today because of his concern. The General had already decided that we should not fly night missions around those mountains, with unlighted airplanes and unlighted air strips.

A young Captain, Richard Schuman, had been Jim's assistant. He was moved up to the position of Division Air Officer, and was soon promoted to the rank of Major. He was an excellent officer and Artilleryman. He did not like to fly very much, so the coordinating job was a natural for him. He said at one time something like: "All you have to do is to fly one of these things long enough, and it will get you." He may have been right. We had enough incidents to make a good case for his point of view. Richard had some other views that, while perfectly logical, did not fit with my approach to flying and the jobs to be done. He was something of a Dudley Do-Right. We were doing so many things on an ad hoc basis that I concluded that there was no right way.

Chapter Fourteen

THE CADILLAC AND THE AIR MEDAL

We at the air strip acquired General Jonathan Wainwright's Cadillac. How did we know it had been his? The Japanese had left the registration slip in its place in the vehicle. They clearly had used it, but they abandoned it when they retreated to the hills. One of our pilots (I don't remember which one) came across it. It had been wired so that a key was not necessary to turn on the ignition and start it. We considered ourselves lucky, for there are times when using an "official" military vehicle is just not the thing to do,

One of the things we thought of to do with the Cadillac was to visit the night life we had heard about in the town of Tarlac. Tarlac is located about half way down the river and valley of the same name on the way to Lingayen Gulf. The supply and support branches, such as Quartermaster, Ordinance and Signal were located there. There was a myth current, reinforced by public relations efforts, that the forces of the rear had only one object in life. That was to serve the boys at the front, and to be sure that they lacked nothing that could be supplied by heroic efforts, if necessary. We did not believe that myth. Military supplies of all kinds were frequently found in the black market. Sometimes, for instance, our aviation fuel did not reach us. We would ask for truck gasoline from the motor park. That would work for a few days, then we would begin to have fuel flow problems. We were told that there was something about the difference in the chemistry of the gasoline that was hard on the fittings on an airplane. Uniforms, food and other things seemed to filter into the black market.

Another feature of the supply base was not a fault of the system, but a natural outgrowth of the war economy. Night life flourished in the city of Tarlac. This is what we wanted to sample. Sitting in the dark for a couple of hours and then retreating to our cots or sleeping bags on the ground got pretty old. It was rumored that there were good restaurants, shows and bars in Tarlac. We hadn't felt that it would be appropriate to travel in a military vehicle for such an evening out. The Military Police agreed with us on that.

One evening five of us got together and went to Tarlac in the Cadillac. We had a rather mild evening, sampling the wares of the bars and of a good restaurant. Some of the Filipino food dishes are very good. I think we went to a live show of some kind, but don't ask me what it was. We could have dipped more deeply into the flesh pots of Tarlac, but, as far as I know, none of us did.

We tooled down the highway, back to our area. Unaccustomed as we were to such "off-base" privileges, we had not given a thought to a pass or any other way to re-enter the combat zone, in which we lived. Of course, the highway was guarded at night. We were stopped by a very serious member of the Military Police. Where are your passes, he asked. Passes? We had none. Here were five Lieutenants who obviously had been drinking quite a bit. They were in an unauthorized civilian vehicle, with no permit to be out of the combat zone, and no authorization to re-enter the zone. If you were a Military Policeman, what would you have done?

The MP actually was kind to us. He took our names, ranks and the identity of our military units, and let us pass. We were home safe, except that for knowing that something would be done with the information that the MPs had. Of course, they would report us to our commanding officers. Oh, well, we would have to explain our behavior.

The next morning, Fred Kutisch and I were told to report to Colonel Nickell, one at a time. We looked at each other, thinking that we knew what was coming. Col. Nickell was one of the really good guys, and here we had embarrassed him, which made us feel like heels.

When we were shown into the Colonel's office, he said absolutely nothing about the caper with the Cadillac. The reason he wanted us one at a time was that he was asking us whether we wanted to volunteer for a mission. An Infantry unit was pinned down, and out of food, water and ammunition. Division

Headquarters had decided that one way to help them was to have an air drop of the needed supplies. We were e ch to have a volunteer in the rear seat to drop a bundle of the needed items, as we dived in low over the isolated Company. He emphasized that we did not have to do this.

Not all pilots volunteered for the mission, though Fred and I did. There was one Battalion commander who did not ask his pilots to volunteer, for whatever reason. I think that one or two others did not volunteer for their own reasons. I tried not to count noses. Anyway, a reasonable fleet of us was loaded up with volunteer passengers prepared to drop the supplies. Each volunteer in the rear seat had a well-padded bag filled with ammunition, water and field rations. It was scary, but no one was hurt. The operation was successful.

For most of us, it was our first Air Medal; that would come later. At that time we did not know that we had been recommended for it.

There is a sequel to the story, however, that is not quite so romantic. I don't know about other soldiers' experiences, but I usually found that many of these exciting incidents had sequels that were definitely anti-climactic, to say the least. In this case, the MPs had not only reported our names, ranks and units, but our possession of the Cadillac. We were soon informed that our possession of it was unauthorized. We knew that, of course. We were further told that it was Army property, having been captured from the enemy. Further, it had to be officially catalogued and classified, to be retained in an official pool of captured materiel. So be it. A few days later we observed some of the Headquarters staff driving around in General Wainwright's Cadillac. So much for unauthorized use of captured materiel.

Captain Bob Munyan also had a Cadillac. I at first thought that it might be ours, after the MPs had taken it from us. Not so. It was a limousine, while ours was a modest sedan. Captain Bob was proud to drive it around headquarters. We, the 40th Infantry Division, were transferred to General Eichelberger's 8th army for the Central Philippines (Visayan Group) invasions. General Eichelberger was also attracted to the limousine. In fact, he liked it so much that he had it shipped to his headquarters in Tacloban.

Chapter Fifteen

LUIGI'S FIRST FLIGHT

While we were using the taxi ways at Clark Field for landing, we also used the revetments for parking our airplanes. They were earth works about five feet high, in semi circles, with open ends large enough for taxiing the airplanes and parking. They would provide protection from bullets or shell fragments coming from any direction except from directly above. It's not that we were attacked that frequently, but there were raids or shelling attacks from time to time. We would not have built these revetments ourselves, with the large amounts of earth and bulldozer time required, but why not use a free gift?

I have reported before that we had assistant crew chiefs who were not trained mechanics, but they could do a great deal of the other work at the air strip, such as fueling, moving aircraft, setting up and taking down living quarters and driving the vehicles issued to us. One day I had our new assistant with me at my airplane.

His name was Luigi, with a surname that I cannot remember. He was a conscientious worker and a good soldier. One day, as he was working with me, he mentioned that he had never been in an airplane. I had a routine "look and see" mission coming up, so I invited Luigi to come along. He kept on his helmet, as we had no intercom, so that he did not need ear phones. He brought his Carbine as well.

After completing the survey, I headed back to the field at a decent altitude, something like 1000 feet. I don't remember whether Luigi or I spotted him first, but a Jap Zero appeared, and he was headed our way. What do we do? As he approached, I went into a tight turn to the left. The turning radius of an airplane varies directly with the weight and speed of the craft. I don't remember any formula for it. Some of the supersonic jets have turning radii of eight miles. One advantage the Zero had over the American airplanes of World war II is that it was lighter and could fly slower, and thus could turn inside of the American's radius. I could outdo our attacker on both counts, light weight and slow speed. Remember, the L-4, or Piper cub, has a stalling speed of 38 miles per hour. It weighs 680 pounds empty. With 12 gallons of fuel, mostly spent by then, my 135 pounds of weight, an Artillery radio and Luigi, we still weighed less than the Zero and its single pilot. And we were slower.

So, our new-found friend the Zero circled, but we were circling inside of him. He would have to be head-on to get us in his sights, and he was not having any luck at that. He could slow down a great deal. That put him very close to us. I could see his eyes, when the sun was not reflecting off his goggles. He had on a cloth helmet. He had a mustache. We looked at each other. Who was going to "blink?"

The Jap blinked, in a way. That is, he left our tight little formation. I knew that I was not home free, however. All he had to do was to get far enough away to turn and get us in his sights, and follow our turns with smaller turns, because of his distance from us. He could then close on us rapidly, because his cruise and maximum speeds greatly exceeded ours. He was also very maneuverable, as U. S. fighter and bomber pilots knew well.

I could have gone into a spin. However, the airplane is out of control until you recover from the spin, and I chose to maintain control. I closed the throttle and pushed the stick forward, putting us into a steep dive. The red-lined, or never-exceed speed of the Cub is 144 miles per hour, which is ridiculous, because you cannot get it to go that fast without diving at full throttle. With power off, I don't know what speed we reached; I didn't have time to look at any gauges. The wing area is so large for the weight of the L-4 that it is hard to hold enough forward pressure to keep it in a dive. All I had to do when reaching tree-top level was to relax the forward pressure, and we were skimming along almost brushing the trees. As we slowed down, I applied enough throttle to keep us going toward our landing strip at a good pace. Again I do not remember which one of us spotted him first, but the L-4 has all around Plexiglas, so vision to the rear is good. The Zero pilot had located us and was closing in on us.

The speed required for a three point normal landing is so slow, that I chose to not waste time, but to land on the main gear wheels. The taxi way was earthen, and uneven enough to aid in slowing, once the main wheels were down. Flying every day, I was able to make the L-4 do just about anything I wanted it to do. I gauged the touch down point and speed so that the end of my roll out came just as I turned into the revetment, and was able to stop short. Luigi's weight in the rear seat was a help that I needed, as, with tail wheel and mains, nosing over is a hazard when making quick stops.

After the landing roll stopped, I did not have to tell Luigi to get out of the airplane. I followed him quickly. Luigi went to the top of the embankment and pointed his Carbine toward the oncoming Zero. I flopped down against the bottom of the embankment, out of the way of any slanting fire that might come from the Zero. I yelled to Luigi to get down and seek cover, too. He did so, after I yelled at him a couple of times. The Jap went over us without firing a shot.

In war, there are many ambiguities. They bother you, but decisions have to be made instantaneously, as was my decision to get Luigi down and into a safe spot. There is a slim chance that he could have hit the Zero with his carbine. If he had, he would have deserved a medal. I certainly would have put him in for one and he probably would have gotten it. My great concern was, however, to get him out of the way of the machine gun firing that I believed would certainly come from the Zero. Was I right to convert him from a potential hero to a "stay alive" advocate like myself? I will never know.

It must be agonizing to command troops in combat. I had very little occasion to give directions, except to fire direction centers, and this did not directly put anyone at risk except the enemy and any civilians who might be in the way. A company, battery, platoon or squad commander must put people at risk every day, or decide that they should not be put at risk. Learning to live with that is an agony I did not have to endure. This one instance is enough to convince me that I would not want to command troops in battle. I have a couple of instances to relate later which bear on this question.

Chapter Sixteen

MANILA

W e, the 40th Infantry Division, were left at Clark Field and Fort Stotsenberg to contain the Japs in their mountain caves and trenches. The First Cavalry Division, coming up the Tarlac Valley on our left, passed us on February 1st and joined the 11th Airborne and 24th Divisions to take Manila. I had not much awareness of that campaign. I have told about the sergeant in the L-5 who evacuated wounded soldiers from that battle.

I was able to get a three-day pass or furlough from my duties with the 40th some weeks later, so I decided to see Manila. I have no recollection of the means of transportation that I used to get there. Nor do I remember where I stayed in town. The sights, sounds and smells of Manila were so impressive that all else was erased from my memory. However, my log book shows that I made a flight from San Fabian to Manila on February 13, 1945. San Fabian must have been the village near Fort Stotsenberg where we set up a strip and quarters. The log book also shows a flight from Manila to San Fabian on February 15, so I stayed over two

nights

—First, the city was torn apart by the fierce fighting. Buildings and streets were in ruins. Especially was this true of the old walled city, called Intramuros. Here a large number of low income Filipinos lived. The Japs had holed up there, and held 4,000 of the residents as hostages. The place had been pulverized. "Collateral damage," that as yet unused term, describes a lot of what, tragically, had clearly happened. Downwind from Intramuros the olfactory evidence was disgustingly present. The rubble was so thick that body recovery was not yet complete.

A panoramic view of Manila

In the whole city, 100,000 Filipinos were said to have lost their lives. Admiral Iwabuchi had 17,000 Navy personnel, who fought to the death in one month, from February 3 to March 4, according to James Jones.[12]

I visited Santo Tomas University, which was a walled city, also. Civilians, Americans, Europeans and others, had been interned there since the Japs first reached Manila. Conditions were terrible, and there was no reason to punish these men, women and children who had done nothing to deserve this.

The destruction in Manila was considerable.

Starvation and near starvation were evident. I am told that the ration was one handful of rice per day per person. Filipinos risked their lives to sneak food over the wall to the residents. This is the only way many of the residents were able to survive. They were extremely thin, and afflicted by many ailments associated with malnutrition. I saw a few of them. They were being well fed by Filipinos and U. S. Army personnel. The well ones gained weight and spirit rapidly. I now know a lady who lived through this experience, who says it was horrible. This was another instance of how the enemy earned the contempt that we had for them.

The city was struggling back. The spirit shown by the residents was remarkable. The "Jeepneys" which became a prominent part of the street scene were not in evidence yet. After the war, surplus U. S. Army Jeeps were purchased and decorated with fancy cushions, fringes on their canvas tops and garish paint jobs. They became the taxis. When I was there, the taxis were "cartelas." They were two-wheeled buggies drawn by single, small, horses. They got around rather rapidly, and the fare was reasonable. The food was good, and reasonable in price. There was no evidence that any vendor was taking advantage of war-time scarcities or the naiveté of the American soldier. Everything was available at reasonable prices. Citizens went out of their way to give you directions, or even to show you around. In all, it was a pleasant break from combat, in spite of the horrors of Intramuros and the other destruction in the city.

Chapter Seventeen

TO TARGET OR NOT TO TARGET

A rtillery discipline places a priority on enemy sites as appropriate targets. It will vary with the number of suitable targets available, ammunition supplies, etc., but there is a preferred priority list. First, a solid enemy installation, such as a warehouse, fortification, railroad or rolling stock. Second would be artillery or mortar positions that were either firing on us or in position to do so. Next would be lighter physical items, such as trucks, tanks or personnel carriers. The story above about the ammunition dump illustrates the principle that some targets are so critical and large that heavier bombardment is recommended. In that case, Naval Air was available and was effective. Machine gun emplacements would come somewhere after artillery or mortars. Caves or other forms of defilade would be in there somewhere. Almost always last in priority would be foot troops in the open, though this might depend on their closeness and the menace that they represented.

Having no other targets in sight, one day I called for artillery fire on troops in the open, apparently digging trenches. Artillery fire scattered them. I did not see any casualties, though some may have been injured but mobile. I did notice something significant. They had tools, but no weapons. By inquiring later, I learned that the enemy we faced had Korean civilians held captive and used them as labor battalions, to do such things as dig trenches, caves and foxholes, and to move ammunition. Thereafter, when I saw them at work, I searched diligently for a target with higher priority. I was always able to find such a target.

The Artillery was very accommodating to our need to discourage being fired on. Exceptions would be made to target priorities if we wished to return fire coming from any enemy quarter One target gave me a great deal of trouble. An enemy anti-aircraft gun fired at me. I immediately called for artillery fire. I mistakenly thought that I could stay just below the cloud overcast and be safer ducking up into the clouds if the ack-ack came too close. This is what happened. I was close to calling for "fire for effect," having completed the adjustment on my target. A strong updraft caught me and pulled me up into the clouds.

One must be aware that the L-4, being a Piper cub, had absolutely no instruments for "blind" flying. There were three engine instruments: oil pressure, oil temperature and tachometer. There were three flight instruments: altimeter, air speed and magnetic compass. There was nothing to tell the pilot whether he is upright, banking, turning or in whatever position. The proverbial "seat of the pants" does not work without visual reference. The inner ear, the organ of balance, becomes totally confused. Lieutenant Fisher, from whom I had inherited the airplane, had acquired a turn and bank indicator and installed it with a Venturi tube mounted outside to generate the vacuum to run it. It was then called a "needle and ball," but its modern counterpart is called a "turn coordinator." When Lt. Fisher went to the First Cavalry, he removed the turn and bank indicator and took it with him. I was staring at a hole in the instrument panel.

I could tell, by the fact that the compass was spinning, that I was spiraling. My inner ear messages were all confused. I could tell that my nose was pointed down, because the tachometer showed increased rpm. And the air speed was building up. To confirm this, I looked at the altimeter. Surprisingly, it was showing an increase in altitude! This meant that the updraft was stronger than my descent caused by the nose-down attitude. The pressure on the seat of my pants confirmed that I was being pushed up, but it was a confused sensation.

How would I straighten out and regain control of the aircraft? I left the throttle at cruise position, to have one constant around which to build my straight and level flight. I concluded from the direction the compass was spinning that I was turning to the left. Thus right stick and rudder should be applied to level my wings. Had I been wrong, I might have gone over on my back and fallen out of the clouds. That might have been a good way to get out of the clouds, except for two things. First, the engine would not run in an inverted position. Second, the Zambales Mountains were close, and I did not want to fall into them.

When the compass stopped turning, my wings were level, but my nose must have been pointed down, for my speed increased. The excessive speed caused the nose to rise. This had to be checked, or the nose would have risen above level flight, starting a porpoise-like motion. I guessed when level flight was approaching, and after a few tries, achieved level flight with the tachometer settling down to cruise rpm. The altimeter soon began giving a constant reading. The throttle being still at cruise, my altitude remaining constant, I must have flown out of the updraft. Everything settled down. Then I looked at the compass again. I was headed toward the mountains! A turn of 180 degrees was needed. How could I tell my degree of bank? How could I monitor my turn to be sure it was 180 degrees? A modern airplane has what is called a direction indicator (DI), which is a gyroscopic compass. The magnetic compass has leads and lags when the aircraft is turning, depending on whether you are turning left or right, and whether you are turning toward north or away from north. I can never remember the combinations. Anyway, I put minimum pressure to the right on stick and rudder, to keep from over banking, and to watch the compass come around with minimum lead or lag. When I decided to stop turning, I had achieved approximately a turn of 180 degrees, and was going away from the mountains. That took a long time. A standard rate turn takes one minute to turn 180 degrees. I must have taken two minutes with my minimum rate of turn. All time seemed long in those clouds. The altimeter told me that I had gained a net 600 feet into the clouds. I must now think of descending, once I had guessed that I was away from the mountains. I saw a hole in the clouds below me, and ground that I recognized. But then a U. S. bomber flew across that hole. My question was: "How many of those folks are in here with me?" A little thought told me that they would not be in the clouds this close to the mountains. This one must be in the clear, and either approaching or departing from Clark Field, which we now fully controlled, so I let down below the clouds. I had told the fire direction center that I was having a visibility problem, and I now called them back. I resumed calling artillery shots and completed the mission. I gave them no further information, and they didn't ask.

A little knowledge is usually a dangerous thing. In this case, more knowledge might have frightened me into inaction. I have since learned that even instrument rated pilots cannot tolerate a "loss of vacuum." This causes their turn coordinator, attitude indicator and gyro compass to fail. They are said to be helpless then and fall out of the clouds. I had none of those things to begin with. A recent seminar I attended told of a report that indicated that, in 1954, a study of 20 cases of non-instrument rated pilots entering clouds recorded an average life expectancy of 178 seconds. The longest survivor lived 8 minutes. You see, I was not supposed to survive. A later, 1985, study showed half of them surviving. Still not encouraging. But, you see, I did not know all of that, so I survived. It is partly due to the maneuverability and ease of flying of the L-4. It does not stall out easily, without letting you know that it is going to do it. It can be handled gently or roughly, and it responds in predictable ways. It saved me; I did not save it.

I later learned that flying just below the clouds is not as smart as I had thought. The enemy will find it easy to get the range to the cloud base. Then all he has to do to hit you is to get the deflection. I had already learned another reason. Up to that time, I had not experienced the updraft phenomenon under the clouds. Clouds sometimes build vertically, when the air is unstable. Strong updrafts occur, building towering cumulus and sometimes thunderheads. Violent storms result. I now stay strictly away from the base of any cloud that appears to be building vertically.

There are objects and installations that definitely are not targets, examples of which will be recounted later.

Chapter Eighteen

HOW NOT
TO FLY

Newsmen and news photographers were not much in evidence in our battles. The battles probably were not as significant, in the whole picture of the war in the Pacific as were Manila, Okinawa, Iwo Jima and Guadalcanal, which were much more exciting stories. An exception is the one story I have related, wherein we gave General MacArthur Clark Field for his birthday.

I do remember one visit by a news photographer. It was while the battle for Clark Field and Fort Stotsenberg was still very hot that I flew this photographer. He wanted battle shots from the air. There were certain precautions that I and the other pilots observed. After all, the General had said that he wanted us alive. We, too, wanted us to be alive. Unnecessary risks were not good tactics, as well as not being good for our first priority, which was, indeed, to stay alive.

This photographer was fascinated by certain artillery bursts in enemy territory and so he wanted closer shots.

They were bursts of shells containing white phosphorus. That material burns with intense heat and emits clouds of white smoke. It is used to set the target area afire, or to smoke the enemy out of his hiding place. The bursts and smoke clouds showed up beautifully on black and white photos. The result of the photogenic nature of these bursts was that the photographer urged me to get closer and closer. I was not at my usual low, protective altitude. Once I had flown over enemy territory, this resulted in some anti-aircraft fire. I should have been flying in a way to prevent that. In any case, when one of the bursts came close enough to rock us, without our being hit by fragments, the photographer decided that he had enough pictures. I was glad to retreat from a position in which I should not have gotten myself.

Another very hazardous flight came as we were leaving the area. We were being replaced by another unit; I believe that it was the 43rd Infantry Division. Officers of the replacing unit were examining the area. I flew a full Colonel over the front. There is a rule in both civil and military flying that the pilot is in command. It is he who must make the go or no-go decisions, for the safety of the airplane and its occupants. At that time it was not a widely known rule in the branches of the Army that were not Air Corps. When there is a full Colonel in the rear seat of the L-4, it is rather hard to enforce that principle.

This Colonel said something like this: "Lieutenant, I want to fly down there." He pointed to the front lines, which consisted of a ravine with our troops on one side and the enemy on the other rim. I replied with something like this: "Colonel, I never fly down there." I explained briefly that high trajectory stuff, mortar and howitzer shells passed above where would have to fly, and flat trajectory stuff like rifle and machine gun fire went over the ravine below where we would have to fly. The Colonel replied to the effect that we would fly down there. I gave in, though I should not have done so.

We went down the ravine, staying above its rims, where rifle and machine gun fire was going by. We could hear it, and see the tracers of the machine gun fire. I don't think any of it was aimed at us, but I couldn't be sure. Above us we could hear the shuffling noises of mortar and artillery shells. It was a delicate flying job. Soon the Colonel could see the folly of our ways. He said: "Lieutenant, I have seen enough." I said nothing, but kept adjusting the altitude at which we flew. The ravine sloped down hill from the mountains to Fort Stotsenberg, on the plain. I had to be careful to stay between the overhead and underneath fire; I was too busy for conversation. When he declared more loudly that he had seen enough, I had to reply. I said something to the effect that I could not go right nor left, up nor down. I would have to fly all the way along the front, down to the Fort.

I have already said that I got no bullet holes in any airplane that I flew in the Pacific and the Philippines. I have reported earlier, in an article on Philippine experiences, that I got bullet holes in my airplane, but none in me. That was the result of faulty memory. As I give these experiences more thought, I realize that the patched bullet holes always were the result of someone else's flying, not mine. It is a great marvel that I got none that day. That was a flight of extreme folly. I determined then that the rule of the final authority of the pilot would have to be followed in the future. I was fortunate in that the commanding officers that I had recognized and respected the rule that the pilot is in command when in the air. The few flights that they made with me were pleasant.

Chapter Nineteen

THE CHEVROLET, THE GUITAR AND AUSTRALIANS

W e were called back to the Lingayen Gulf and we camped near the town of Dagupan. We entered training and staging for our next operation. Our destination was supposed to be a secret, but we soon knew that we would invade the Island of Panay, which was also the Province of the same name.

When we lost the Cadillac back in Bamban, we had an ace in the hole. We also had a Chevrolet, similarly liberated from the fleeing Japs. We were discreet about that, in light of what happened to our Cadillac. We kept it hidden in the boondocks and seldom drove it.

When we moved to Dagupan, someone drove it for us down the highway and past 6th Army Headquarters in Tarlac. I don't know how that was done, but then I wasn't supposed to know. We kept it hidden at Dagupan. It had been sighted, however. It was definitely "hot." The Military Police were looking for it.

One day a young soldier came strolling by the air strip, with a guitar on a sling over his shoulder. Our Captain Petry knew how to play a guitar, and he was curious about this one. He told the soldier that he admired his guitar. The captain asked whether he would consider selling it. The soldier asked the Captain how much he would give for it. The Captain said: "I'll show you." He took the soldier to the hiding place of the Chevrolet. The soldier said: "No, you wouldn't trade a car for a guitar; you're kidding." The Captain replied that this was easy to explain. We were to be shipped out in a week or two, and would not be able to take the car with us. We may as well get something for it that we can take along to our next station. He did not mention the fact that the Chevrolet was hot. Of course, he hadn't been asked that question. The soldier went away happy, driving his new prize. We saw him driving it around for about two days. Then we saw MP soldiers driving it. Obviously, we had not issued a warranty with the sale.

We had pleasant evenings while we were training. The prohibition of lights did not apply to the area of Lingayen Gulf by then. We had more spare time, because the training routine called for few observation flights and no artillery firing. We sat around in the evenings singing familiar songs and making up words for familiar tunes. We meant no disrespect toward the Filipino guerrillas, for they were extremely helpful, but we had verses about them and their zip guns. In one, the chorus went something like this: "For I'm a brave guerrilla; got a cigarette, Joe?" Guerrilla was pronounced in the Spanish way, the way the Filipinos pronounced it. It sounded like "guerriya,"

We saw a group of soldiers in a stockade. They wore regulation fatigue uniforms, but had no insignia of rank, nor did they have any Army unit designations on their uniforms. I asked someone who they might be. The answer was: "Australians." I then asked why they were being held in this way. The answer was that they, too, were stationed on New Britain Island when we were there. When we loaded up to go to the invasion at Lingayen Gulf, they took off their uniforms and put on ours, and they shipped out with us. No more dull days in the New Britain jungle for them! It seem incredible that some commanding offices had these undocumented soldiers in their units without being aware of it. There they were, however. They got there some way. The Australian Army now wanted them back. Apparently our commanders were assuring the Australian Army of their return, by keeping them securely confined until they could be transported. This reminds me of a history of Australia which characterized the earliest English settlers there as "transported" prisoners. After American independence, America apparently would no longer accept "transported" prisoners, so a new land was found for them. One of the ironies of history is that Australia subsequently became he most law-abiding country in the world.

Chapter Twenty

PANAY

I do not remember a thing about our loading up and sailing south for our next mission. It is said that we loaded on March 12 and embarked for Panay, one of the Visayan group in the center of the Philippine Islands. In is also said, in the same source, that we landed twelve miles west of Iloilo, the capital city of the province of Panay.[13] Perhaps I don't remember the sailing trip down the islands on the LST because I didn't make that trip. I learned from General James Delk that our L-4's were loaded onto C-47s and flown to Iloilo. I may have ridden along in one of the C-47's. I do remember several flights in that reliable work horse of the Pacific. Anyway, our mechanics unloaded them and set them up on the airfield north of the city. We had them flying very soon, but I don't remember the specifics. Our excellent mechanics came through again. We didn't have a lot to do, as there were only a little over 2000 Japs on the island. The guerrillas had things under control on most of the island.

In this smaller society, things became clearer to us about what had happened and what was happening.

There was in circulation, in the province of Panay only, a Filipino currency, with a special war time designation. It stated on the face of its bills that the U. S. Treasury would redeem it in Philippine pesos, or in U. S. dollars. Fortunately it did not say how many dollars. The story we heard was that the Colonel in command of the guerrilla forces had been authorized to issue a certain amount of these war pesos, and the U. S. Treasury would redeem them at the pre-war par of one U. S. dollar for two pesos, up to the number of pesos authorized. The hitch was that the Colonel forgot to turn off the press, and ten times the authorized amount was issued. This amounted to a loan from the civilian population; payable when the pesos were redeemed. Since there were these excess numbers of wartime pesos, which caused them to depreciate in value, it amounted instead to a tax on the population to support their armed effort. Prices quoted in those pesos reflected this inflationary issue. Prices in dollars were reasonable, but in these war pesos, they were about ten times what you would expect.

I later got another graduate degree and taught Economics in several universities for about 35 years. In Principles of Economics courses, you teach that there is such a thing as the "Quantity Theory of Money." This says that a change in the general price level will occur in proportion to a change in the quantity of money in circulation, other factors being constant. Other factors are seldom constant, so that the student has a hard time seeing the application of the theory. I simplified this story and used it to teach the Quantity Theory of Money in my classes. I pointed out that "other things," like the amount of goods and services produced, certainly could not increase in proportion to the number of pesos chasing the goods. Very likely the quantities of goods and services decreased in war conditions. That would have made the inflation even worse.

General Eichelberger, 8th Army Cmdr., pins the DSC on Col. Marcia Peralto, guerilla leader on Panay. General Brush, who read the citation, is at the left.

We were on Panay, near Iloilo at two times, both before and after we took back Negros Island. I am not sure in which tour some of these things occurred. Probably the second, because we landed on Negros Occidental on March 29.[14] However, we did not transfer our air operation to Negros until two days before the capital of Negros Occidental, Bacolod, was secured. We moved to a field we created in the village of Guimbal on

111

the island of Panay. Here we blocked off a section of paved road and used that for a landing strip. We built a detour around our strip with a little bulldozer action.

Panay guerilla leaders in conference with Division Intelligence (G-2)

I'll relate the story of the DDT spraying here. Someone designed and someone built a spraying device for the L-4. By removing the rear seat, we could install a tank in its place that held about as much liquid as we would want to carry, with 65 horsepower. Pipes with sprayers were mounted on the wing struts. We had a control valve. There were baffles in the tanks so that the sloshing effect was bearable.

We didn't know at that time that DDT was bad for humans, for the wildlife, and other things. It was the wonder pesticide of the time. We were to spray Iloilo and surrounding territory. Flies and Dysentery were scourges on Panay. The infant mortality rate was horrible. Soldiers were not immune, and neither were adult Filipinos. Mosquitoes were also a menace. We were to be the public health heroes.

I think that we only had spray equipment for one airplane, though my memory could be faulty on that. In any case, since I had had some experience with crop dusting type flying, I either volunteered or was picked for the first application of DDT. This is really low and slow flying. You have to be low enough that you don't get a lot of scatter, but get the material on the targeted areas. Going under a wire rather than over it may be the safest way to go, in some circumstances. I do not remember going under any wires on that job. I do remember making crop duster turns at the ends of rows. A standard rate turn of 180 degrees will take one minute, and you wouldn't be lined up for the next pass, for the radius of the turn would exceed the width of a pass. By pulling up to a partial stall and doing a wing over, you can change direction 180 degrees in ten or fifteen seconds, and be in line for the next pass. You then regain flying speed by pointing the nose down. You level off just above the row to be covered.

Crop dusters usually have flag men to mark the rows. These persons move over the width of an application pass each time. Of course, they get much more of the spray than does the field, because they are under every pass. The pilot is supposed to keep the spray turned off until he passes the flag man at the beginning of the run, and shut it off before passing over the man at the end of

113

the run. That may or may not work well, as there is a lot of over spray. We didn't use flag men. We had to "eyeball" each row and move over the right distance to assure even coverage, with little overlap and few gaps. How well did we do? Passably well, I think.

After my first load, the Air Officer, Major Schuman, told me that those turns were dangerous. I'm afraid that I replied with something as ungracious as "It may depend on who is doing them." Any way I'm afraid that I didn't mend my ways. My log book shows that I sprayed DDT on three days: July 21, 23 and 27.

There is a somewhat amusing and slightly embarrassing sequel to the spraying episode. A couple of us were invited to dinner one evening at the home of a prominent Iloilo business man and his family. They had three daughters at home, of teen age and older. I had noticed, while spraying south of town, a rather imposing looking establishment with several substantial buildings. While I was spraying the site, a lot of girls or women came out and waved to me. They used handkerchiefs, towels and even their skirts to wave. The last should have been a clue, but I didn't catch on. I asked the girls in the home where we were being entertained about that institution or establishment. They would only giggle. Their father explained to me that it had been a Tuberculosis sanitarium, but was now out of use for that purpose. The medical authorities of the U. S. Army were using it to rehabilitate prostitutes with diseases. Dumb me. I had to ask.

The Iloilo, capital of Panay Province, as we saw it. This is our airstrip.

I remember three more flights made during that period on Panay. The 40th, reinforced with the 503rd Airborne Regimental Combat Team, invaded Negros Island a few days after we landed on Panay. The Division Air Section stayed on the field at Guimbal for a few days longer. We didn't move until two days before Bacolod, the capital of Negros Occidental, was secured. Then we moved the base of our operations to the city airport of that town.

The enemy, numbering only between two and three thousand, had moved into the mountains of Panay, so there really wasn't much of a ground war on the island of Panay. The Air Officer asked me to explore the western half of the island. I was to fly north in the

115

center, which consisted of a fertile plain, with mostly rice cultivation. There is a town called Capiz at the north end of the plain, near the north shore. I was to turn there and fly back along the coastal plain adjacent to the western shore of the island.

We did not have proper aerial navigation charts for any of the islands. MacArthur's battle maps were excellent, but they were of a scale and detail that was not helpful to flying. We used road maps. Navigation by road map is difficult and imprecise at best. I couldn't really get lost, if I followed the shore home. However, I underestimated the time that the trip would take. If you will recall, I said that the 12 gallons in the L-4's tank would last three hours at the consumption rate of four gallons per hour. I have since consulted the specifications for the L-4H, which we had. It shows a burn rate of 4.06 gallons per hour. So, if you really stay in the air three hours, you are on the proverbial "fumes" for the last three minutes. Of course, things are not that precise. The amount of climbing you do, the gentle or rough way you handle the throttle, weather conditions, and a host of other factors affect the precise burn rate. In any case, you had better be on the ground before three hours are elapsed. The Army did not allow us to do one thing that would be normal for flight. The mixture control is a critical element in flying, especially when you change altitudes. You can economize on fuel by leaning the mixture. More important, the efficiency of the engine at high altitudes requires leaning to offset the effect of thinner air. The Army's thought was that we were flying at low altitude so much of the time that we would not need to lean. Besides, we had no cylinder head temperature gauges, and so we might overheat the cylinders and burn valves

I began to realize, coming down the western coast of Panay, that I would have trouble getting back to the base at Guimbal. I had landed at the only airport that had been on my route, but there was no fuel there. A landing and a takeoff consume more fuel than cruising, so I was really in trouble. I could cut across and go over the mountains, but the enemy occupied the mountains. Besides, I was instructed to look along the coast for any unfriendly activity. So, I had to proceed along the coast. I cut as many corners as I dared.

To make a long story short, I landed at Guimbal after exactly three hours of flying. How much fuel did it take to fill me up? Just a little short of 12 gallons. I had seen no enemy activity to report They say that negative intelligence is as important as positive intelligence. For the risks I took, I hope so.

Another flight that I remember preceded our occupation of Bacolod, the capital city. An Artillery Captain was in the rear seat as observer. The Artillery was in place south of the city. What they wanted was for us to register their howitzers on a base point and check points in the city. We flew from Guimbal and arrived over Bacolod. We checked in with the fire direction center. The center gave us the coordinates of a street intersection and asked us to adjust the fire on that as a base point. We looked on the battle map and found the intersection. Adjacent to the intersection was a building with a red cross on it, on the map. We looked on the ground, found the intersection, and, sure enough, there was a red cross painted on the top of that building. What were these guys thinking of? That was a hospital! The Captain and I looked at each other. Shortly he picked up the mike and said: "Unable to observe." The fire direction center replied: "You pick one."

We looked and looked. One thing typical of Philippine cities is the abundance of people on the streets. I am told that most Asian cities are like that. We found an intersection adjacent to the provincial capitol building. There were wide lawns surrounding the capitol. This would be a good place for some of our "over" and "deflection right" rounds to land. We gave the coordinates of that intersection and waited for fire direction to plot it and fire the first round. There were still a lot of people in jeopardy. We got out a message pad and wrote on it: "Go to your air raid shelters." We dropped it in a message bag, which has a weight and a long orange streamer. We saw people read our message. About half of them were believers. They scurried away, presumably toward shelters. The other half just looked up at us and went on their ways.

When we met some of the people later, they said that Japanese soldiers who were there, but in the shadows, so that we could not see them. They scoffed, saying something like: "Those little airplanes can't hurt you; they are radio controlled." They were angry at those who sought shelter, threatening to set fire to the shelters.

When the first round landed, it fell harmlessly on the capitol lawn. Then everyone was a believer. Scrambling was the order of the day. It was amusing, in a ghoulish way. The ponies drawing the cartelas could be persuaded to speed. The ponderous water buffaloes pulling the clumsy, solid wooden wheeled carts could not be convinced. The drivers were beating them vigorously, but with no effect. Anyway, by the time a round landed in the street, virtually no one was there. We talked to several of the people who had been there. They reported that no one was hurt. Of course, the escapees from our artillery shots included the Japanese soldiers. Suppose that we had fired on the crowd. What would have been the ratio of civilians killed or wounded ("collateral damage," in more modern, euphemistic language) to enemy soldiers killed or wounded?

The Captain and I did not report this aspect of the mission. When does the court martial begin? What we did was strictly against military protocol. But, as I have said earlier, the hell of war seemed a little funky from our altitudes. You could observe all kinds of action in slow motion, and you could affect some of it. There were no hills or high ground near Bacolod, so that the fire direction center was dependent on the L-4's for most of their observation and adjustment of fire. This meant, too, that they were not observing what we did or didn't do.

There was another memorable flight from Panay to the city of Bacolod. I was alone on this mission. I was expected to fire the artillery on some targets in and around the city. It must have been 25 statute miles across the water between the islands, for my round trip flights, without any observation missions, logged at 50 minutes. At 70 miles per hour, that would be 35 miles each way, and our strip at Guimbal was ten miles from the nearest point of land. I started with full fuel, but was asked to fire several missions. Finally I said something like: "I'll have to go now; my fuel is low." I would get an answer like: "just one more short mission." "O. K., I'll do it, but this is absolutely the last." This happened again. Then I really had to go across the water. I had done some slow flying during the missions, so I had a little more than three hours of fuel, but I had no way of telling how much more.

I headed out over the water. I had no choice, for we did not yet have a secure place to land on Negros. I couldn't lean, but I could slow-fly. This would increase the time spent in agony, but it would conserve fuel. I did not head directly for our air strip, but to the nearest point of land. Then I flew along the shore. If the sand were wet, it would make a good landing place. If there were only dry sand available above the water, (at high tide), at least I would have a relatively benign place in which to nose over, which was better than the jungle. I then sneaked in over the trees to our road landing strip. On landing, I found a pilots' meeting in progress. While in the meeting, I was approached by our assistant mechanic (the Luigi of the pursuit by a Zero). He whispered in my ear: "Lieutenant, I put in 12 gallons." This was not my last bout with near fuel exhaustion.

Chapter Twenty One

BACOLOD

The landing at Palupandan on Negros and the subsequent advance to Bacolod, the capital city of Negros Occidental, proceeded so smoothly that the advance troops found General Rapp Brush and his Aide de Camp Captain Robert Munyan sitting in their Jeep on one of the main streets of the city when they arrived.[15] This was enjoyable for General Brush and Captain Munyan, but embarrassing for the troops and their commanders. It makes me feel more confident of our earlier decision to warn the population before we registered the Artillery on an intersection of the city. Could it be that General Brush and Captain Munyan were in the city at the time we registered on that street intersection? Certainly, at the least, there was a distinct lack of enemy troops to shoot at.

We established our Division air strip operations on the Bacolod city airport. The ground crew set up tents there for their quarters, supply tents and operations office. The pilots were quartered in a summer resort type hotel in town. We all ate with Division Artillery Headquarters Battery. The artillery battalions and

121

Infantry regiments were in the mountains, pursuing a fleeing enemy. The fighting got tough, as they approached the enemy dug in positions in the mountains. My Battalion, the 143rd, was located on a ridge overlooking the coastal plain. We constructed a small air strip there, for the purpose of picking up observers, or for the rare occasions when the commander or some other officer needed to get into Division Headquarters.

Life was much better for those of us quartered in town. Many fine families entertained us. We learned what it was like to live under Japanese occupation. It was not nice. There were some collaborators, however. At each of the parties we attended there would be some U. S. Service persons in uniforms without rank or unit insignia. They were the Military Counterintelligence guys. They were interested in the civilian guests. They wanted to determine who was a collaborator, what was the degree of collaboration, and whether they presented any danger to us at this time. Later I had a friend and colleague who had served in this group in the Philippines. He found that there were a lot of degrees of collaboration. It was natural for a family with financial or other interests at stake to want to get along to a certain degree with the occupying authority. There were some difficult decisions to make. The Filipino hosts could not have been nicer to us, whether they had been reluctant collaborators or not.

I remember one flight from our battalion strip on the ridge. I climbed to some altitude, to get a view over the mountains. Foolishly wanting to conserve fuel and time,

I glided power off all the way down to the strip. In the tropics, we let the discipline of using carburetor heat in reduced power flight lapse. We thought: "How could I get carburetor ice in this climate?" It was not hard at all. The air is very humid, and temperatures can be reduced 30 degrees or more in the intake throat of the carburetor. At altitude, temperatures are lower than the usual 80 degrees of Philippine days. I landed without incident. A few minutes later, taking off for another flight, I had a near power failure on takeoff. I regained full power and landed. I panicked and called the base for a mechanic. A pilot had to take the time to bring him out. Thorough examination of the engine and its accessories found no problem. The unanimous conclusion was that I had landed with ice in the induction system. Sitting on the ground, it had melted, providing a healthy dose of water on my takeoff. I felt foolish, as well I should have.

There were some flying incidents at Bacolod. We had a replacement pilot, freshly trained and sent over to do combat duty. Flying with only road maps was a bit of a challenge for him. The Americal Division was at Dumaguette, the capital city of Negros Oriental. Dumaguette was at the southeast corner of the island, while we were near the northwest corner. The flight to Dumaguette was a stretch for an L-4. Our new pilot, "Junior," was sent to Dumaguette on some kind of mission. He was to return alone the same day. He must have fueled while there, for one could not hope to make the round trip on 12 gallons. He lost his way on the way back. You would think that it would not be possible to be lost on an island. The island is big enough, and clouds usually surround the peaks that are the backbones of these volcanic islands. Therefore, one can become confused, as he did. I know why he became confused that day. There is a pass through the chain of volcanic mountains that is the backbone of the island. It was filled with clouds that day, so he flew over the top. At the necessary altitude, the L-4's engine was less efficient due to no leaning ability. There was a strong wind from the North. In order to get to the coast and away from the overcast, which was an undercast to him, he flew west. When there is a solid undercast, you cannot tell that wind is drifting you. When he came down at the coast line, it was strange to him. With only a road map, and that with virtually no details for that part of the island, he was lost. He realized that he did not have enough fuel to make it all the way to the base in Bacolod. He did not come back We received word that he had left Dumaguette. So, early the next day, the Air Officer sent me out to look for him. I flew most of that day, with several re-fuelings. My log book shows seven hours of flight that day. That's a lot in a Cub, as any Cub pilot will affirm. I found no trace of Junior. We were sad. I don't remember whether anyone was sent out the following day. On the third day, in walked Junior. He had come up the coast in a local sailing vessel. He had decided to land. He found a field big enough for a landing, but not for a takeoff.

He went back by Army Landing Craft Mechanized (LCM) with a mechanic, and they took off the wings of the L-4, towed it to the coast, loaded it on the LCM and brought it back to Bacolod. That was not a glorious beginning of his tour with us. However, we were glad to see him return safely.

I should say something about the LCM or "M boat," as we called it. It was just about big enough for a 2 1/2 ton truck, a tank, an armored vehicle or an armored personnel carrier. It had a flat bottom, no keel and a square prow. The prow lowered to make a landing or loading ramp. Many people who were not in the category of "brass" were carried around the islands in M boats. The motion of the boat, with flat bottom, no keel and square prow, was such that one was seasick before leaving the harbor.

Chapter Twenty Two

PURSUIT

Guerrilla forces controlled about two thirds of the island of Negros. That made the task of the reinforced 40th Division easier, until the enemy was cornered in its mountain hideouts. Then it was the same grim task we had faced outside Clark Field and Fort Stotsenberg. That was to contain them and try to force them out, to surrender or be killed. They mostly opted for the latter. Our services, as Liaison pilots, were critical from the first. One job was especially unique to us. That was to pursue the enemy units in the flights of their ground units, to find out where they were going, and find routes for the ground forces to get to them.

I remember one search mission that was mine. I was to fly out in a certain direction and try to determine where a Jap infantry unit had gone. They had been sighted, but their trail had been lost during the night. I flew along in the indicated direction for half an hour, seeing nothing of military nature. Then I spotted what seemed to be a platoon of guerrilla forces walking along a road. I dropped a message to them. It said: "Take out two telephone poles; I want to land and talk to you." It

127

General MacArthur visits General Brush. Unidentified staff officers in the background.

A 155mm battery of the 222nd F.A. Battalion with an L-4 headed for the target area

128

was not easy, but they promptly took out the two poles. I landed on the road. Mabuhay was again the greeting. I expressed equal pleasure in seeing them. They had an idea where the Jap infantry had gone, and when they had passed through the area where we were. I had the information I had been sent to get. I thanked the leader of the platoon, shook hands with as many guerrillas as I could, and took off from the makeshift landing strip and headed for the base at Bacolod. I did not look back to see whether they replaced the telephone poles!

One pursuit mission turned out badly. General Rapp Brush seemed to be a fine soldier and commander. We liked him. We believed him to be a West Point graduate, as were most generals in the position of Division Commander. General Brush had been directed to capture a saw mill on the north end of Negros Island. Army Headquarters wanted lumber. I don't know whether he had actually been directed to use the Paratroopers of the 503rd Airborne RCT attached to us. Probably he had merely been expected to use them, as they were available. I can't imagine that General Brush would have violated direct orders. In any case, he did not use an air drop. The reasoning that we heard was that any air drop would result in a certain number of casualties, due to the nature of the exercise. How many lives should one expend for a sawmill? He used the 503rd Parachute Combat Team, but in ground action only. The troops did not get to the mill promptly enough The Japs had burned it. We heard that the General was severely criticized for not making an air

An M-7 tank fires on enemy positions.

130Bombed out enemy supplies.

drop. The mill was salvageable, however. The equipment was still usable, and lumber was cut as soon as a crew could be assembled.

General Brush was not the favorite of General Kreuger, Sixth Army Commander. In preparation for the invasion of Japan, the 40th Infantry Division was again assigned to the Sixth Army. General Brush was called back to Washington, given a physical examination, and retired. He was old enough for an honorable retirement, which he deserved and apparently got. However, we hated to see him treated in this way. The date given in the history for the retirement is July, 1945. This is more than one month after the sawmill incident. This leads to the conclusion that the mill incident was only one of the quarrels with General Kreuger of Sixth army. We respected General Brush, but not his successor.

One unpleasant task remains in my memory. Before reaching their mountain hideouts, some elements of the Jap forces put up resistance on the edge of the coastal plain. The Division decided to call in air assistance. I do not remember whether the air that they called for was Naval or Air Corps this time. Anyway, the Air Officer directed me to fly a path marking the front lines of our troops. They asked for close-in bombing of enemy positions but a few yards from our own troops. I flew what was indicated. The bombs were dropped. Our forces complained about the closeness of the bombs to themselves. I could very well have flown some distance into enemy forces. I flew over enemy forces almost every day. My instructions were to fly on the line marked. The bombers may have dropped a few in short of the line. I think that was the case in one or two bombs. I do not know whether there were casualties on our side. I was afraid to ask. Some of those missions were uncomfortable.

The Japs everywhere seemed to behave in unacceptable ways. Being conquering forces, one might not expect them to be lenient. However, it is hard to understand the gratuitous cruelties inflicted by them. On Negros, there were stories of a Colonel Watanabe. The local people called him "the laughing killer." There were stories of his killing civilians at random. He would walk down the street, and on a whim, take out his sword and lop off the head of a civilian. He would then laugh a ghoulish laugh. Should we have believed such stories? I don't know. He was one of our very few captives.

Colonel Watanabe was willing to be cooperative. He promised to point out locations of Jap units in the mountains, if we were to fly him over them. This was not so that we could kill them, but so that we could, with Colonel Watanabe's help, persuade them to surrender. I was very glad not to be assigned the mission of flying Colonel Watanabe. I did not trust his oily manner with us. What if he decided to become violent in the air? A pilot can very easily be over powered from the rear seat. Of course, whatever happens to the airplane and its pilot, happens to the rear seat passenger, too, when they are in the air. What if he were suicidal? That was a realistic possibility, as most Japanese seemed to prefer death to capture. The flights with him in the rear seat went off without incident. I was still glad that I had not been asked to fly him.

Watanabe is not an unusual Japanese name. There may have been lots of Colonels Watanabe in the Philippines. A year or so after the war, I read of a Colonel Watanabe who was convicted of war crimes in the Philippines.

Chapter Twenty Three

THE
FOUR DOCS

After we had secured Clark Field and the mines had been swept, we left our grass shack in Bamban and moved to quarters between Clark Field and Fort Stotsenberg. There we occupied a middle class type of house that was more comfortable. We flew from the taxiways of Clark Field. Heavier Air Corps airplanes used the runways. We didn't need them, as the taxi ways were perfectly good for our purposes.

Division Artillery was assigned a medical officer, a Captain whose name I cannot recall. It's just as well. As a medical practitioner, he was said to be a good poker player. I did not play poker, so I cannot attest to that. We called him simply "Doc." He said that he had been a practicing physician on an Indian reservation in Oklahoma.

The rank of Captain was normal for medical officers. I do not recall ever seeing one with less rank. An Artillery officer would have to serve about two years, and command a battery or hold a responsible staff position to earn the rank of Captain. Medical officers, by virtue of their M. D. degrees, were initially given the rank of Captain, if not higher.

We teased all "medics" somewhat about sick call. It was claimed by soldiers and officers that on alternate days the medic would give you a pink or a white pill, no matter what your complaint. We thought this applied especially to the Doc. One of us would greet him: "Hi, Doc, which is it today, pink pills or white pills?" His reply would be unprintable.

Doc was definitely "nervous in the service." He was what we called a foxhole jumper. Everywhere he went, he dug a foxhole. The rest of us should have been more conscientious about that; we sometimes did and sometimes we didn't. Doc liked to spend time at the air strip. Not that he wanted to fly. "What, put my ass in one of those rickety things? No sir!" What he liked was the absence of brass and the somewhat funky atmosphere. There was too much formality at Headquarters, and there wasn't much to do after sick call.

Doc would jump into his foxhole at the slightest disturbance. I have mentioned that we now had a middle class type house with glass windows. Peasant houses have no glass in their windows. They have shutters to keep out the night breezes and stray bats, but in the day time, breezes and all go right through the house. Doc had dug himself a nice foxhole just outside the window from our operations room. One day an enemy plane came over. Doc jumped into his foxhole. The trouble was, he went out the window, forgetting that there was glass there. He got a cut.

We persuaded the Air Officer to put Doc in for a purple heart. It was awarded to him.

There was a medical officer with Division Headquarters who had a sharply different approach to life. He was not only not "nervous in the service," but he was courageous in other ways. We did not call him "Doc." We called him Major ... whatever was his name.

While we were on Panay, a Roman Catholic priest came to him for help. The priest said that the people in one village for which he was responsible were dying. He wanted medical help. The Major visited the village. He reported to some of us what he found and what he then told the priest. He found that the villagers, like some of the more remote dwellers outside of the main stream of Filipino life, did not use latrines. Their houses were built on stilts, and a hole in the floor served their toilet needs. Scavenging animals did what clean up was done.

The Major said that he spoke sharply to the priest. He told the priest that, being educated, he knew all about fly-borne contagious diseases, and that he should have guided his people to better ways. The Major said that the priest responded that he "only looked out for their souls." The Major then told the priest that he would have no souls left if he didn't apply some of his knowledge. He directed the priest to secure shovels and lime. He was told that our Army could supply the lime, if he would get shovels. He should teach these villagers to dig latrines and use the lime to keep the flies away. The Major was undoubtedly a force for positive improvement in the life of the island, but only a drop in the bucket compared to what needed to be done. The dreary funeral processions with the tiny coffins were so much in evidence on this island that it made one cry.

While in Bacolod on Negros, I met two Medical Officers of the rank of Lieutenant Colonel. Each had a unique approach to the practice of military medicine. One was a medical authority in the Division. He operated an institution that was very useful to military personnel. It was a regulated medical facility in which the prostitutes operating in the city were examined regularly and treated. In fact, their operations were confined to one hotel, if that could be possibly enforced. It was a great service to the military, because the amount of lost time to venereal diseases was large. The soldiers seemed to have little judgment in this regard. (I'm implying that the officers' conduct was more prudent. I think so, but I'm not sure.) This is the same medical officer who must have been responsible for the facility on Panay, just south of Iloilo.

At one time a C-47 made a landing on our strip and crashed. The strip was the municipal airport, and long enough, though it was very narrow. The pilot ran it off of the strip and damaged it. The engines, wings and instruments were taken away, leaving the fuselage at the side of our strip. Within two days it was a brothel. Girls from a spot like that were rounded up and placed in the controlled facility.

To illustrate the irresponsibility of some of the soldiers, I'll cite the case of one of our assistant mechanics. This occurred while we were on Luzon. He went to a village that was notorious. He came back with a case of Syphilis. Only a few years before that, it would have been incurable. The army could cure him, but he was off work for a week. We had no excess help. Someone had to bear the burden of his task. What did he do? He went back to the same place and contracted the same disease. Therefore he was out another week. This is another reason I was glad not to be a commanding officer.

There was one medical officer from the hospital that was with us on Negros. His rank was Lieutenant Colonel. I met him briefly one day at the air strip. I knew him by his patients. I knew two young men who had received the circumcision operation performed by this medic. Now there may have been good medical reasons for the operation. The tropics had its own medical risks. However, I knew of no other case in the armed forces where the operation was performed as widely as it was said to be performed in Bacolod. The Colonel was not making religious conversions. He simply liked to recommend and perform the operation. I wondered about him.

Chapter Twenty Four

HARD TIMES

One of the positions which I did not envy was that of troop commander in combat. There were losses in every campaign, and a commander had to feel these losses, and to wonder whether he could have done something differently, to prevent some of them.

One battery commander in one of the battalions had his own way of reacting to the strain. When his battery was in reserve, away from the fighting, he would remain in his tent, dead drunk. The General intended to ask the battalion commander to relieve him of his command. Fortunately, this was the general with all the common sense and humanity. He thought to ask the men in the battery in question about their commander. I don't know what they said to the General, but the gist of it was that they pleaded to have him remain as their commander. They said that he was terrific in combat. He knew what he was doing; he knew how to instruct and encourage them. They felt secure under his guidance. He took care of them when they felt that they needed it. They did not need him when in reserve. Let him do his thing. The

General had the good judgment to listen to the men. He did nothing and that Captain served out the war in command of his battery. Later, when the war over and we all went through the separation process at Fort Lewis, Washington, the Captain got drunk and missed the train that was to take him home. That was no longer a military problem.

Another battery commander had an experience while in reserve that was quite different. They were actually in the city of Bacolod, enjoying being in reserve and the sights and entertainment of the city. The city was not immune to infiltration at night by small groups of Japs bent on destruction. One night a Jap soldier made it into the parking area of the howitzers. He had explosives strapped on his back. He wrapped arms and legs around a howitzer and detonated the charge. He was blown to bits and the howitzer was damaged beyond repair. One life for one gun. What a calculus! That's the way they were.

The Captain commanding the battery did not escape. He was blamed for not having adequate security guards posted. I hope that the news that we got was not true. What we heard was that a court of inquiry had determined that the Captain would have to pay for the howitzer. Monthly deductions would be made from his pay check.

I don't know exactly how long our airplanes had been in the Pacific area, but it had been at least three years by the time we were at Bacolod. In those days the fabric covering of the fuselage, wings and tail surfaces was cotton cloth, shrunk to fit and finished with nitro-cellulose dope. There never had been any shelter for them. That period of time sitting in the tropical sun made the fabric rotten. Our ground crew had materials and the skill to make patches, but neither the amount of fabric needed nor the workplace to completely re-cover the airplanes. The engines were in need of top overhauls. This would be equivalent to a ring and valve job on an automobile engine. The crew did not have the facilities to do that, either.

Our solution had been to order new L-4s. The order had gone in previously, while we were still on Luzon, and nothing had been heard from it. The Army Air Force was our supply arm, and their Philippines base was in Tacloban, on Leyte Island.

The fabric situation got so bad that, one day when I was flying my commanding officer, Colonel Knowlton, from the battalion strip to the main strip in Bacolod, fabric ripped off of the upper surface of the right wing. Two sections, each about three feet in width, came off and blew away. The Colonel, Stewart Knowlton, understandably, was a little nervous, as he saw the fabric fluttering down to earth. The Cub, or L-4, has so much excess wing surface for its weight that I was able to fly tolerably well with that much surface gone. A lot of cross controlling got us into the base without difficulty. Our excellent ground crew had an adequate patch on it before the day was out. Stewart Knowlton had replaced Colonel Nickell as Commander of the 143rd Field Artillery Battalion when Nickell was transferred to

Divarty Headquarters. Colonel Knowlton was also a fine office and a gentleman.

That right wing by now looked battle-weary. Junior officers and enlisted men were required to carry a carbine on the left shoulder at all times. As pilots, we had gotten permission to carry the 45 caliber pistol that was standard for senior officers. There was no issue of shoulder holsters, so we had them made in civilian shops. A side holster hung from a belt would have been very awkward in the cramped space of the seats of an L-4. We would caution officers and men to take that carbine off of the shoulder before walking under the wing. Sometimes we would forget. The muzzle of the carbine would poke a hole in the underside of the right wing. If the Carbine bearer were tall, or on his entry into the rear seat from the right side, no matter how tall or short he might be, a hole would result. The underside of the right wing had all of those little round patches. One could easily tell someone that they were bullet holes, and be believed. The six foot long patch on top of the wing was visible, for the crew had run out of olive drab dope, and had only put clear dope on it.

One day, not long after my wing incident, the Air Officer told me to be ready at eight a. m. sharp the next morning to transport a visiting officer from the Pentagon over to Iloilo. I replied that I certainly would be ready at 8:00. I wanted him to know, however, that I had an artillery mission to fire for my Battalion at 6:30. I would tell the Battalion, and be sure to complete it in time to be back by 8:00.

At 6:20 the next morning, I took off for the Battalion strip. There I picked up a Captain as an observer. We flew over the target area and completed, I think, two artillery missions. We came back to the Battalion strip. The Captain got out and went on about his business. The space was so limited on the ridge where the Battalion and the airstrip were located that one battery fired directly across the strip. As I prepared to fly back to town, the battery was firing another mission. On the artillery net, I asked for them to hold their fire while I took off. Their answer was: "Wait." I tried two more times and got the same answer. I was not going to take off into that fire. Depending on the nature of the target, they might be using proximity fuse. Thus a round would not have to hit you to burst and fill you full of shrapnel. So I waited. At five minutes to eight, I was given the "all clear." It was a ten minute flight to town and the waiting brass.

At eight o'clock promptly, the Major was on the air. "969, where are you?" (969 was my tail number and call sign.) "Five minutes out," I replied. "Report to me at once." "Yes Sir." I replied.

The Major, our Dudley Do-Right Air Officer, kept me at attention and chewed me out for what I thought was too long a time. He did not ask the reason for the five minute delay, so I did not give him one. "No excuse, Sir." The Major had once said that he thought his main job was to keep the brass happy. He seemed to be trying to do that. He was showing all of this brass from the Pentagon that he ran a tight ship; no tolerance for a Lieutenant who was five minutes late. The Major's priorities did not agree with mine at all. My first priority was to stay alive. My second was to fly the airplane well. I thought that these two were closely related. My third priority was to be a good artilleryman, and thus serve my commanding officer well. I thought that I had been true to all of those that morning. I had little room in my priorities for keeping brass happy. My observation was that they did a pretty good job of taking care of themselves.

What further ticked me off was that the group of, I think eight, senior officers from the Pentagon and our Major and our Captain and other pilots stood around jawing for another twenty minutes after the Major was through with me. I was assigned a tall, very trim, full colonel as a passenger. He was a nice enough fellow. He was extremely neat, with new, well pressed uniform. I wore a frayed, wrinkled flight suit, canvas jungle boots and a baseball-type cap made by a Filipino tailor from an old khaki shirt. Because of the earphones we wore, we could not wear standard head gear, and the fatigue caps issued did not have long enough bills to protect us from the tropical sun.

On seeing my airplane, the Colonel asked: "Lieutenant, are you sure that this airplane is safe?" Now this was a standard question that we got from non-flying personnel. It was meant as a jest, to put the pilot at his ease. The standard answer was: "Yes, Sir, these are very safe airplanes." That answer was meant to put the passenger at ease. I answered, instead, "No Sir, this god damned airplane has had it." I could see the Colonel looking at the patch on the upper surface and the little round patches on the under side of the wing. They certainly supported my rude statement.

In a case like this, we were expected to seat the passenger, see that his seat belt was fastened and caution him to stay away from the controls accessible from the rear seat. Then we were to strap ourselves in the front seat and wait for a crew member to come along and hand-prop the engine. However, as we often flew alone, we had a solo starting procedure. We would prime the engine by pulling it through several compressions with the throttle cracked and the magneto switch off. Then we would completely close the throttle and turn the switch on. Because there was no hand brake to set, we would place one foot in front of the right main wheel, reach the tip of the propeller from behind and snap it through one compression. The engines were so well tuned that they would start that way. With the propeller in the closed position, the idle was very slow. Those Continental A-65 engines had hydraulic valve lifters. One had to rev the engine up to 1000 or 1200 rpm in order to fill the lifters with oil, so that the engine would run smoothly. Otherwise, there would be loud clacking noises, and the valve action would be erratic, causing loping and uneven firing. For this occasion, I left the throttle closed. The engine clattered along, occasionally causing the whole airplane to shudder, with drumming noises in the wings.

The Colonel and I waited that way, being the last to

147

take off in our little convoy to Iloilo. The others formed a ragged formation at some decent altitude, like 3000 feet. Not so, for this young Lieutenant and Pentagon Colonel passenger. I flew along, low and slow, just above the waves. The waters in the Islands were very clear. One could see turtles as big as large dining room tables, and sharks even larger. I would point them out to the Colonel. He was very silent, for some reason. On arriving, he thanked me politely and joined his comrades. I flew directly back to Bacolod, without standing around to jaw with anyone.

It was only a few days later that we received a telegram telling us that our new airplanes were in the supply base at Tacloban. I credit myself with inducing an inquiry into where were the new L-4s that had long ago been ordered by the 40th Division. I was especially confident of this after we went to pick them up. Supply personnel there told us that they had been there for some time. No one had known what to do with them. No one else gave me credit for finding our new L-4s, for I hadn't told anyone what I had done to the Colonel. So much for keeping the brass happy. I think that I got results by making one member of the brass unhappy.

Chapter Twenty Five

I LEARN
ABOUT FLYING

We received a telegram telling us that our new
L-4s were in storage at the base in Tacloban.
Tacloban is on the east shore of Leyte Island.
We were on the western shore of Negros.   We therefore
had to fly across Negros, across a strait to Cebu Island
and across it to Cebu City.   There we had to re-fuel at
the U. S. Army base in Cebu City.   Then we had to
continue across another straight and across Leyte to
Tacloban. Tacloban has been listed as the second largest
city in the Philippines. We found little to recommend it.
War conditions seem to have caused its appearance, its
sanitation and its general character to retrogress. To be
polite, I'll report that we thought it to be the armpit of
the otherwise beautiful Islands.

Army Air Force personnel at the supply base had not
known what to do with ten "Piper Cubs" arriving in
crates. The thought of looking in the requisition files to
see who had ordered them seems not to have occurred to
them. I still believe that when I made my "Brass"

passenger from the Pentagon so unhappy in Bacolod he had a lot to do with the base finally locating the airplanes and notifying us of their location.

The base personal were not sure of their ability to assemble the L-4s from the crate. We had anticipated that and therefore carried a number of mechanics with us. We stayed over one night. Working the rest of the day of our arrival and into mid morning of the next day, the assembly job was completed. We got to test fly our new L-4-Js late in the morning of that second day.

The difference between the L-4Hs that we turned in and the L-4Js is that the latter had a controllable pitch propeller. The propeller had wood blades attached to an aluminum hub that was adjustable. It had gears at the hub. It was connected to the cabin with a long shaft. The shaft was rotated by a crank and set of gears in the cabin. One could set a fine pitch for achieving a higher rpm for a climb-out, or steeper pitch for lower rpm and a better cruise speed. Thus both for climbing and for cruising we could get more exertion out of the 65 horsepower Continental engine. This meant, of course, that we were forcing more fuel through the engine. Not having an ability to lean the mixture for better performance, this increased fuel consumption was inevitable. The only way to avoid that was to pretend that we did not have the controllable pitch and cruise and climb at the same, neutral, pitch setting. The propeller was called a Robley propeller. It did not work very well, for it was hard to keep vibration down to a satisfactory level. There was enough slack in the system of gears to allow differences in pitch in the two halves of the propeller. The Robley propeller was also provided on Globe Swift aircraft. We were told that it did not work very well there, either.

After lunch we loaded up and departed for "home" in Bacolod. I had an empty rear seat on the trip to Tacloban, so the Major asked me to transport a soldier to his unit bivouacked near the northern end of Leyte. He had been hospitalized and was now ready to return to duty. He had a full duffel bag, which we were barely able to cram onto the rear deck. We were over gross weight, but I did not know by how much. Never mind, the Robley propeller will take care of it on the climb out, I thought.

The soldier's unit (which I believe was a part of the 77th Division) could be reached by going through a pass in the mountains which formed the backbone of the island. The other pilots could skirt the mountains to the South and go almost directly across the island and straight to Cebu City for the fuel stop.

After climbing out, I saw fairly heavy rain in the pass. I did not relish flying through heavy rain. I looked at the mountain ridge. What looked as if it were a wispy cloud was at its top. I thought that I would go over the top. Here I was in an airplane that I had flown for only twenty minutes. I had no idea how much difference in fuel consumption would result from using the properties of that new propeller. I really did not know the rate of climb I could achieve, nor the cruising speed that I could achieve. We had no navigation charts. The road maps that we were using did not tell us how high these mountains were, nor what were the shapes of their contours. I therefore started out with an abundance of ignorance. Lesson Number one can be derived from that ignorance. Do not undertake a flight that strains the airplane's capacity with so little knowledge.

When I reached the top, which proved to be over 4000 feet, I found that there was more than a wisp of clouds there. In fact, there was a solid overcast on the upwind side of the ridge. To me it appeared to stretch all the way to the coast. I thought that by going over the top I would have to fly to the coast, let down, and fly back to find the soldier's unit. There was about a five hundred foot space between the ridge top and the overcast. I thought I could fly through that. I also thought, mistakenly, that as the mountain sloped away on the windward side, I would have higher and higher ceilings until I reached the coastal plain. I was dead wrong. The under side of the overcast followed the contour of the mountains. Never did I have more than a 500 foot ceiling until after I reached the plain. I had to let down at a faster rate than was normal for a power-off glide. I had to switch back and back again, for there were other ridges defining the lateral space I had along the mountain side. In short, I was descending in a tube that did not grow in size. Of course the cylinders on this new engine were cooling faster than they should. Also, there was the danger of the engine loading up with so much idle throttle setting. I had to rev it up occasionally to clear the engine, which made my descent more difficult. I do not know how my passenger was taking all of this. I dared not turn my head, for I did not want him to see the concern that must have shown on my face. Besides, I was much too busy making my tight turns in the 500 feet between the clouds and the trees. Lesson number two: do not enter a tunnel unless you can see out the other end, preferably into sunshine. A turn of 180 degrees was impossible, because I could not climb back up the tunnel down which I was descending. Lesson number three: never enter an environment in which a turn of 180 degrees is not possible. The old reliable 180 degree turn will solve most environmental problems, but not the one I had gotten myself into.

These were three of the worst flying decisions I ever made, and two more were to follow. If I had continued to make decisions of this quality, my flying career might have been a lot shorter than the fifty-five years that it has turned out to be. I have never entered such a tunnel between clouds and mountains since that day. If fact, I have turned around many times in the face of such conditions. I have always made sure that a turn of 180 degrees would be possible. I have always been determined that I must know the performance of any airplane I am flying before attempting anything close to its limits. In the Flying Magazine, there was for a long time a feature page called "I Learned About Flying From That." This flight would have been a good candidate for that page. But wait. There is more.

When we reached the coastal plain, I could see that the overcast did not extend all the way to the coast. I had not flown high enough above it to be able to see its edge. Lesson number four: look carefully at the obstacles before making a decision. I could have gone over the top in great comfort. It is not a good idea to go over the top if you are a strictly VFR pilot and your airplane is equally restricted. If you can see the ground on the other side, however, going over it is a lot better than going under where there are mountains.

We looked for the soldier's unit. We found where he thought it was. There were marks on the ground indicating that a large encampment had been there. Everything was abandoned. After some time, we located the air strip. It was equally abandoned. Flying around a bit, we located two tents and two vehicles. We determined that they were U. S. Army issue. After we flew around them a bit, one of the vehicles started toward the air strip. We went back there and landed. There was no fuel at the air strip. I thought that the vehicle coming our way might have a Jerry can of fuel. On the other hand, a rear-guard party such as this probably had a limited fuel supply. I asked the soldier whether he minded being left there alone. He said no. He probably was glad to do anything to get out of that airplane. Because I was already behind any reasonable schedule and the nine others were undoubtedly waiting for me in Cebu City, I took off without waiting for the vehicle to reach the air strip. Lesson number five: do not pass up the possibility of fuel in favor of a quick departure in order to meet some schedule.

I began to realize that I knew little about my

remaining fuel. Which propeller setting should I use to conserve on fuel? You may know the degree of sophistication of the fuel gauge on the Cub or L-4. It is a wire on a cork. The wire extends out of the vent in the fuel cap. It bounces and sinks until the cork reaches the bottom of the tank. When it stops bouncing, you have very few minutes to a landing, be it voluntary or involuntary. The trick is that each airplane is unique in this last gasp of fuel. The corks have a gasoline-resistant shellac on them. As they age, this shellac permits some fuel to enter and reside in the cork. Thus it gets heavier and becomes more of a pessimistic indicator. The cork in this airplane had been immersed in its first gasoline this morning. How light was it, and hence how optimistic was it as a gauge? I began to worry about this too late, so I headed north up the coast of Leyte, to cross the strait at its narrowest point. I then flew down the coast to Cebu City, in order to have a beach under me for a forced landing, if necessary. Of course, this put me ever farther behind schedule. I would have been better off to wait at the abandoned strip for the possibility of fuel.

On arrival at Cebu City, I found that the mechanic put in eleven and one half gallons. There was one half gallon of fuel remaining in the tank, enough for seven and one half minutes of flying. That was a secret between the mechanic and me. The other pilots were so peeved at me for the delay that they were not speaking. I received the complete silent treatment. No one asked me for my story, so I said nothing. I was not very proud of leaving the soldier alone on that abandoned air strip. Nor was I proud of having gone over the top of the mountain and under the overcast. "Ask me no questions and I'll tell you no lies." So "proud" was I of these dubious achievements that they have not been told to anyone in 53 years until now.

We had a replacement pilot fresh from the States. I do not remember his name. His rank was Staff Sergeant. That meant that he had the same Liaison Pilot training that we had had, but had not had the Artillery background. He had the Tactical Flying course at Fort Sill, so that he was competent enough in the some of the Artillery skills that we knew, as well as recent tactical flying training. He was a good soldier and a good pilot. He flew with no one in the rear seat on this trip. What was in his mind that caused him to stray from our ragged formation going back to Bacolod was a mystery. I certainly did not ask him after we returned. Stray he did, and he became lost. Flying with only a road map was a challenge to him, as it had been to Junior.

When we landed at our home base, a nose count showed the Sergeant to be missing. I do not remember whether I volunteered to go find him, or whether the job was assigned to me. In any case, I strapped a Jerry can of gasoline to the rear seat of that L-4J and set out. I thought that I might find the Sergeant out of gas on a road or in a field. That was not the case. I found him wandering around on Negros, trying to figure out how to read the road map. It seemed to me that simply flying west would have gotten him to the coast, then he could have found Bacolod. It was the only city of any size on the West coast. However, when you are confused, you don't think in such a logical fashion. We returned to our base. Nothing was said to either of us about our delinquencies. I guess that the Major was tired, and wanted nothing more to do with that day's flying. We were happy to have our new L-4s, even though the propellers didn't work very well. We were very happy to have the Sergeant back safely.

Chapter Twenty Six

A ROMANTIC INTERLUDE

There was not a great deal of romance in our lives. I don't know whether I have succeeded up to this point in communicating the boring and depressing nature of war as an exercise. Our days seemed endless. We received very little news from home. Some of it was propaganda in nature, like the news that we had captured Clark Field for General MacArthur's birthday. We only half believed the official news of the war. We did not know how much of our local scuttlebutt to believe. In short, it was a dreary life. The stories I have told to this point would seem to be exciting. They were interludes in long days and evenings in which nothing would be happening, except some of the raids by small enemy groups. I have told about two or three of those. Those were not exciting.

We did have a social life in Bacolod that was the best of the war for us. Local citizens entertained us, as I have reported. We also had a hospital, with nurses among the medical personnel. There was an officers'

159

club, as well as a non-com club and a USO place of entertainment. Our Major Schuman was young, single, and a good mixer, as well as a good soldier. There was a nurse named Penny. Her maiden name has escaped my memory. It does not matter, for her surname has been Schuman for many years.

The romance and the wedding of Penny and Dick was the high light of the social season in Bacolod. There was a large gathering. Two Chaplains were on hand to officiate. There was a reception in a place which was larger than the officers' club. I do not remember what was the nature of the facility, but it was adequate.

I doubt whether they had a lot of time together, for we were moved again, back to Panay. I don't remember whether the hospital moved with us. When, right after the end of the war, we were shipped to South Korea, I simply do not know where the hospital was located. In any case, we know that the Schumans were together after coming home from war duty.

My wife and I had a Christmas card relation with some of the pilots and mechanics after the war. Gradually, as we changed our residence several times, these relations were lost. The Schumans lived in Leadville, Colorado, where he was a banker. That is all that I know about their lives after the war.

There may have been other romances in the lives of some of our men but there was very little opportunity for anything but the dreariness of the war.

Chapter Twenty Seven

POOR SHOOTING

Division Headquarters had developed a routine for use of the L-4s, pilots and observers while we were on Luzon. The practice was continued on Negros. I can recall that the enemy forces on Panay were not large enough to justify use of this tactic. Each morning on Negros, right after dawn, a junior officer from Division Headquarters would come to the main air strip in Bacolod. He would have a target that had been selected at Headquarters during the evening before. This target would be given to the pilot who was assigned for the "dawn patrol" that morning. The dawn patrol had two objectives. It was, secondly, to survey the target area and be prepared to report any new developments or changes since the day before. The first and most important objective was to adjust fire on the target selected at Headquarters.

A central battery of a centrally located battalion would be adjusted on the target. At that time, on Negros, we had five battalions of artillery. Each had twelve howitzers, so there were 60 in all. Though only two guns in one battery would actually be firing the shots that we would request from the air, all five fire direction centers and the gunners on all 60 howitzers would be following all of the commands except to "load" and "fire." In this way, Headquarters would be assured that all fire direction personnel, all gunners, officers in charge and ammunition handlers would be alerted the first thing in the morning.

When we would have the adjustment completed with the two firing howitzers, we would call for "fire for effect" and all 60 weapons would fire. They would have the correct settings, for they would have followed all corrections. The exercise was the main objective of the firing, but a target of significance would have been selected, so that ammunition would not be wasted. The messenger with the target from Division Headquarters would wait for the return of the pilot and the observer, and debrief them.

I was the designated pilot for the dawn patrol one morning. General Hervey came with the designated target. The General himself! This must be a significant target! The General gave me a battle map with a location marked as the target. It was way behind the mountains, where surface observation could not see it. It was deep into enemy territory. Nothing was visible on the map in that area but jungle. When I was confident that I could find the target, I asked the General what was the nature of the target. He replied that it was a field hospital. In some shock, I blurted out: "General, our reputation will go to hell.!" The General just looked at me. I said: "yes sir" and climbed into the airplane. I forgot that you address a general as "yes, General," and not "yes sir."

I flew to my battalion's air strip, as an observer from my battalion had been designated. A Captain McCarthy was waiting and flew with me. On the way to the target area, I showed the marked map to Captain McCarthy. After looking at it for a while and noting that the target was in a remote area, he asked what is the nature of the target. When I told him that it was a hospital, the cockpit was filled with profanity. I added: "That's what the General said." The Captain said: "The General himself?" I replied in the affirmative. No more was said during quite a long flight back to where we could see the target area.

When we arrived in a position to observe, we could see nothing. It was all jungle. By matching terrain details with the map, we could identify the location marked on the map. We proceeded to adjust two guns on that imaginary target. It was imaginary to us, for we could see nothing. It was understandable that the field hospital would be concealed under jungle cover that would purposely be left undisturbed. Shell bursts of the ammunition we used could do damage with a twenty five yard radius, and thus be dangerous for a total of fifty yards. Therefore, standard firing tactics called for getting a shot "over" the target and one "short" one hundred yards apart in range. The deflection, or direction, should by then be correct. Captain McCarthy proceeded to get the over and the short one hundred yards apart, and called for fire for effect. It is up to the fire direction center to decide the type and amount of ammunition to fire.

One round was fired from each of the 60 howitzers. They were supposed to land in a dispersed fashion within the 100 yard bracket that had been established. They did no such thing. They were scattered all over the landscape. We could not even see the two that we had adjusted landing in the established bracket. The standard procedure in a case like that is for the observer to adjust two howitzers from each battalion on the target, and then repeat his call for "fire for effect." This loses some of the element of surprise, but it gets the ammunition on the target. Captain McCarthy and I looked at that sorry display of shooting. He said: "I think we hit O'Reilly's barn.". I turned around to him and said: "Well?" He said, into the microphone: "Range correct, deflection correct, fire effective. Cease fire. End of mission."

We flew back to the Bacolod base. We were glum all the way back. What shall we tell the General? Lying is a serious offense in the Army. Especially, lying in combat is dangerous and serious. Should we continue with the lie and tell him all sorts of thing about hitting that target, or should we admit lying about hitting it?

When we arrived at the Bacolod strip, there was no one there to debrief us. We were off the hook.

That story burned a hole in my conscience for forty years. For the first time, in 1985, I told the story to the Rector of our local church. Only then did I figure it out. It had been so uncharacteristic of General Hervey that it was a great puzzle. Then I thought of it. He was not the senior general in the division. Two of them outranked him. He must have lost an argument over that target. That would explain why he came down to the air strip himself. He did not want to send a junior officer with that kind of message. It also explains why there was no one there to debrief us. He did not want to know what we did with that target.

I regret that I had not thought through all of those implications. When I moved to the Los Angeles area, General Hervey was still active in banking circles. While acting as a teaching assistant at Brown University in Rhode Island, I had in one class a young man named Hervey who bore a strong resemblance to the General. The young man said that he was a cousin of the General. I had the perfect opening gambit. It would have been nice to see the General again, and I flatter myself to think that he would have enjoyed a visit. He had flown with me on many occasions. I dared not approach him, for that target was there and too painful to talk about. I still could not figure out how he had done such an out of character thing. After I told the story, I could do some more thinking about it. Up until that time, it was a kind of black hole into which I dared not go. Further thought offered a possible explanation for that very bad shooting on that morning. In my days teaching gunnery at the Artillery School, I had never seen a student fire as badly as those battalions fired that morning. Of course! Every fire direction center must know the nature of the target, in order to select the appropriate ammunition and the number of rounds to fire. There are enough persons involved with enough measures and calculations in a fire direction center that an error can be introduced at any point that will throw the firing way off. Of course, those people didn't like the target any better than Captain McCarthy and I had liked it. That bad shooting was deliberate on somebody's part. This story illustrates the folly of simply burying a painful story in your mind. Think it through!

A further note on wartime treatment of hospitals and their patients might be in order here. When the 37th Division came to the town of Bayombong on Luzon, they found a Japanese hospital with all of the patients dead. They had been shot, so that they could avoid the humiliation of being captured.[16] There are two other stories of Jap action that I was reminded of in an interview. I now remember them. This was on Panay. Some of the Jap soldiers had acquired Filipino wives and children. When the Jap soldiers retreated to the mountains, large numbers of these dependents were murdered by the Jap authorities. There was a military hospital near Iloilo, containing a number of Japanese soldiers. When the Jap forces fled, they injected something into the patients that made them pass out. Then they set fire to the hospital. We know this because a few were still conscious and fled the fire. These incidents do not excuse any of our behavior, but they add perspective to the nature of the war we were fighting.

Chapter Twenty Eight

HOW TO
IRRITATE YOUR
AIR OFFICER

I may have mentioned the boring character of the active war effort. To the reader, these adventures in the air might seem to make life exciting. Such is not the case. One is reminded of the jaded pilot who once cracked that flying is "hours of boredom interrupted by moments of stark terror." That, to me, describes the life of a combat pilot. You sit around waiting for a mission. There is no reading material, and the jokes and other conversation that flows around soon get old.

Missions that were interesting or exciting were rare interludes in a dreary life. Even flying the L-4, which is really the ultimate in basic flying, tends to be dull when the missions are routine. I was appalled to again notice, from my flight log book, how many of my flights were between Bacolod on Negros and Iloilo on Panay. Even though there were twenty-five miles of shark-infested water, it was boring. The flights were clearly of the courier type once we had secured our Negros foothold and moved to Bacolod. The flights transported what we classed as "brass." Anyone up through the rank of captain who must travel between the islands had to go on the daily M boat, with attendant sea sickness. Thus our passengers were "brass" consisting of Field Grade or General officers. "Rank has its privilege," or RHIP, was a meaningful cliché in the army of that day. Is it still true?

One such courier mission turned out to have its own version of excitement, bordering on stark terror. For some reason that I cannot recall, I was flying someone else's airplane that day. The crew chief had installed a fuel gauge designed for a Jeep. He then eliminated the wire on a cork that is the typical gauge for an L-4 (and still is, for the Piper J-3). That seemed to be a fine idea.

There was one hitch. On returning alone from a courier flight to Iloilo, I had a fuel stoppage about ten miles out over the shark-infested water. I was puzzled because we had been getting our aviation fuel with no trouble. While we were on truck gas on Luzon, such a problem was frequent, but not since we came to the Central Philippines.

Whatever might be the cause, I found a partial solution. Before the propeller stopped windmilling, I started using the primer. It was mounted on the left end of the instrument panel. It had its brand name etched on it: "Lunkenheimer." We called it simply "the Lunkenheimer." One pulled the plunger back, let the tube fill with gasoline, and pushed it forward in the pre-start procedure. This action pumped gasoline through small copper lines into the combustion chamber of each cylinder. Why would fuel go into the Lunkenheimer tube and still not flow to the carburetor? I assume that the suction created by pulling the plunger back was a greater force than the gravity created by the fall of fuel from the tank to the carburetor. There was only about a fifteen inch fall, after all. Anyway, it worked, after a fashion. While I was pulling the plunger back and when I was waiting for the tube to fill, the engine would windmill ever slower, with no combustion. As I slowly pushed the plunger forward, I would get power. This was very inefficient fuel injection. A modern engine, with fuel injection, squirts the fuel into the combustion chamber near the top of the compression stroke, just before the spark occurs. Here I was pushing in fuel also during the power, exhaust and intake strokes as well as during the entire compression stroke. This made for a very rich mixture, and it wasted fuel. I had to push slowly to avoid flooding the cylinders out and killing my power.

In that crippled fashion I made it the ten miles to the air strip. Everyone was alarmed, if not amused, by the sound of the L-4's engine as I approached. I had no altitude to spare, as the power that I was able to maintain was not enough to keep me aloft. The Major was irritated, when he found the nature of the problem. He seemed not especially glad to see me, with this new problem.

It took about ten minutes for me to descend slowly over those ten miles. The thumb on my left hand was so sore that it was a problem. That thumb still tingles when I recall the incident. I thought of going on sick call with it. How would I explain it? I had pushed the Lunkenheimer for ten minutes? Not a likely sounding report. Besides, what could the medics do for it? Would it be a white pill, or a pink pill?

The wire on a cork performed two functions. The primary function, as we saw it, was to give us a bobbing approximate reading of our remaining fuel. A second function was to keep the vent hole open and clean. Maybe that second function was more important than the first. The gasoline and its fumes had caused the gasket to swell and choke off the vent. The vacuum was preventing the fuel from flowing by gravity to the carburetor. The solution was to return the wire on a cork. There was no harm in having two fuel gauges.

The only occasion in fifty-five years of flying that I ever damaged an aircraft was while we used the road landing strip at Guimbal on Panay. (While writing this chapter, I had a main tire blow out on landing. I managed to stay on the runway, but cracked the engine mount in the effort. My second damage to an aircraft.) I turned off the road too quickly and hit a stone. It bent the V holding the main wheel on the left side. It was easy to repair, as we had a supply of such V's. I was not the only one to bend one. Our first Major had borrowed my airplane one day and had bent both V's by hitting a dike at the end of a rice paddy. Air officers are irritated by such incidents, however. They are solicitous about equipment as well as about personnel.

The 503rd Airborne Regimental Combat Team was attached to us, as I have reported. They seemed to have only one pilot and one L-4, though they would have been authorized two of each if it were a full Artillery battalion that was a part of the Combat Team. It may be that it was not a full battalion.

A certain recklessness was characteristic of the flying by this pilot. The Artillery battalion commander was a daring type, and he induced his pilot to do some flying of a type that we had given up doing. Like flying by close to the mouths of caves suspected of containing artillery weapons. More irritation for the Air Officer. No harm came to them, so maybe all's well that ends well.

One of our replacement pilots was not as familiar with short field landings as we had become, what with our practice in the south Pacific and our actions in the Philippines. We had a number of auxiliary strips near the combat areas. On landing on one of these rather short strips, our new pilot over-ran the strip and wiped out the landing gear. The propeller was miraculously spared, so the damage was not severe. Landing gear parts were expendable, in our operations. Each aircraft carried a book of forms. Form 1-A was the pilot and passenger record. The pilot's flight pay was authorized by entry in the Form 1-A. The form 1B was the aircraft record: the discrepancies and the corrections, signed off by the crew chief. The pilot also had to sign off on discrepancies and enter any damage. This pilot duly entered the incident, and under "remarks," said: "This airplane has a definite over-shooting tendency." That was amusing to most of us, but not to the Air Officer.

One day, out of sheer boredom, I listened to an itinerant peddler of pet animals. I bought from him a monkey on a leash. The price was right, and the creature looked appealingly at me. It turned out that the monk was not well received at the hotel where we were quartered. I left him tied up at the airstrip. After about two nights, the animal escaped and disappeared. I suspect collusion in that escape. I had no regrets, as that ape belonged in the wild, not on an airstrip.

Fred Kutisch and I found one excellent way to irritate Major Schuman. When we moved back to the island of Panay, we found a shortage of bamboo there. To strengthen the squad tents in which our ground crew lived and in which we kept supplies, the crew had fashioned pole frames. This greatly improved the living quarters and made them stable in winds, and better able to shed water in the heavy rains that we had. How were they to do this without bamboo? We could have tried to have the poles shipped on an M boat during the move, but that would have required paper work and a doubtful approval. Fred hit on a solution, and I followed him. We each took four poles and lashed them to the landing gear of our L-4. The large end would rest in the X formed by the main gear struts. The small ends would be lashed together and tied to the hand hold near the tail surfaces. The lashing had to be secure against the 70 miles per hour cruise speed. It also had to prevent the poles from going forward into the propeller during landing. It all went well. The flight characteristics seemed to be improved by the presence of the poles. The irritation factor was noticeable, however.

Chapter Twenty Nine

LOSSES

I have mentioned several replacement pilots without indicating why we needed as many replacements as I indicated. I have reported the death of Jim Williams, our first Air Officer. Then Lieutenant Fisher transferred to the First Cavalry Division. While in the Central Philippines, we had one loss due to illness. I hope and believe that he recovered, but he was no longer with us. There was a replacement for him whom I never met. He was with a regimental combat team that was detached from us for two missions. The 108th Regimental Combat Team was detached for the purpose of finishing up the suppression of Japanese troops on Leyte, and then to wage the campaign in Mindanao. Anyway, I remember the report of the death of this pilot. He received a gunshot wound while flying a mission. I do not recall whether his observer was also hit. In any case, the pilot made a crash landing back at their air strip. Whether from the gunshot wound or the crash, or both, the two were killed. I recently received a report of an observer killed in a flight operation on Negros. My memory does not contain that incident, but I accept it as true.

Of the pilots, then, the casualties were two killed and none wounded. The were eleven of us in the full complement of the 40th Infantry Division artillery. There was one more in the attached Airborne 503rd Regimental Combat Team. If we call our full complement twelve, the loss of two by death is a loss of 16 2/3 percent. I don't know whether that is high or low, compared to other types of service. I suspect it is low compared to Infantry and certainly compared to Infantry in the Marine Corps. Such arms as Quartermaster and Judge Advocate General must have had much lower loss percentages, so that the overall loss for the Army and for the armed services engaged in combat must have been lower. This inquiry relates to the popular impression that the Liaison Pilots, in their flimsy, unarmed, low flying aircraft were unusually exposed. It is my belief that we were in about an average position from the point of view of risk. The total strength of the 40th Infantry Division for the Philippines campaigns was 15,838. A total of 758 were reported killed. This is about a 5% loss to death. There were 2030 Purple Heart medals awarded.[17] On the assumption that the Purple Heart was awarded to those killed, and to all of those injured, the number 2030 represents the total casualties. This means that there was a 12.8% casualty rate for the Division. To my knowledge, none of us pilots received a combat wound, except for those killed. Thus my recollection places our casualty rate only slightly higher than that for the Division as a whole.

We did have one replacement pilot who remained

with us to the end of our assignment. He is the one who arranged the reunion in Peoria, Illinois, that I reported earlier.

I do not know how many members of our group now survive, 53 years after the end of our ordeal, or adventure, whatever one chooses to call it. As I have said, we kept up a Christmas card correspondence for some years, but all of those contacts were lost in our many moves through graduate schools and teaching assignments.

Chapter Thirty

LIEUTENANT, I'VE SEEN ENOUGH

Quite often we could be of direct service to Infantry units and their officers. A view of the combat zone from the air, at low altitudes, could enable an officer to better grasp the tactical situation. He could assess more accurately the dangers facing his unit, and he could select tentative paths to safer or more effective positions for his men.

Near the end of our duty on the island of Panay, I flew three such missions in one afternoon. There were three Infantry Lieutenant Colonels at the air strip. By their rank, I took them to be battalion commanders, though they could have been senior staff officers. They seemed to be directly concerned for Infantry troops in the field, so I imagined that they were commanders.

The situation was the following: The Japanese troops, long ago defeated on this island, had retreated to an area of low mountains, hills and valleys. They subsisted there, mostly by raiding isolated villages in the hills and valleys for food and water. They were not much of a menace, but they were troublesome. You could not simply forget them. They were armed and they still had ammunition. They raided us at night, and they were definitely a hazard to the villagers. Several of our Infantry units were tied down in the task of containing them. We were training for the invasion of Japan, but we could not ignore this more immediate duty.

I took one of the Lt. Colonels up and flew over the area of the front between our troops and the enemy. We got close, so as to observe the details of the tactical situation. We got a little too close, for the enemy opened fire on us with rifles. We could hear the "pop" of the rifle, then a "zing" as the bullet passed by us. Then one came by with a "zap." The Colonel was an Infantry officer, so he knew what that meant. It meant that that last one was close. He said: "Lieutenant, I have seen enough." I thought that that was a good decision. We went back to the air strip.

I took up the second Lt. Colonel. (We used the abbreviation for Lieutenant in this situation, and called them "Light Colonels.") We proceeded as we had with the first Lt. Colonel. As we got closer, for a better look, we heard the "pop" followed by the "zing" and then by the "zap." The response of the Lt. Colonel was amazingly like that of my first passenger of the day. He said something like: "Lieutenant, I have seen enough." So, back to air strip we went. I was not sorry. Twice in one day is enough to be a target, so I thought.

The third passenger was waiting. Why was I

designated to take all three of them? The reason for that is gone from my memory, if I ever did understand it. Anyway, we proceeded as before. We got close again, because it seemed important to the Lt. Colonel to get a good look at the front and the Infantry on our side, as well as the position occupied by the enemy. I never did know which of the troops might be the responsibility of each of the officers. Anyway, we received the same sequence of enemy fire. Need I repeat it? I think not. Amazingly again, the response was almost exactly the same. I probably do not remember the exact words, but their import was: "Lieutenant, I have seen enough." Not reluctantly, I took us back to the air strip. That was the end of my work for the afternoon.

My log book is not capable of telling me which date was the day on which I made these flights. In that period, just a few days before the Japanese surrender, I made from one to five flights every day. All three flights probably did not total more than one and one half hours of flight time.

Skipping over time to the days of my return to the United States after the Korean tour, I'll relate my discovery that a personnel clerk had mistakenly put the award of a Bronze Star on my record. When I saw this, I knew that no one had ever awarded me a Bronze Star, so I looked in the file. There was a Personnel Order with my name at the top, along with the names of the three Lt. Colonels I had flown that day. The names at the top simply designated whose files were to receive copies. Reading down, I found three paragraphs that were almost identical. Each read something like this: "For flying as an observer in a Liaison aircraft, disregarding his own safety, over enemy territory and experiencing enemy fire, in order to better assure the safety and effectiveness of troops under his command, Lt. Colonel ____ is hereby awarded the Bronze Star for bravery in the face of the enemy." Each of the following two paragraphs read about the same. I do not have the words exactly, but they were standard award language. Fair enough.

Looking down the pages, I found a paragraph relating to me. It read something like: "For completing twenty five missions flying a Liaison aircraft in the vicinity of the enemy, in disregard for his own safety, First Lieutenant Donald A. Moore, O-1177101, is awarded an Oak Leaf Cluster to his Air Medal." Again, fair enough. The ratio of 25 to 1 did not particularly bother me. What would I have done with an Oak Leaf Cluster for every time I had been shot at?

We expected officers of the rank I flew to be awarded Bronze Stars. We called the Bronze Star "the field grade officers' good conduct medal." I will explain the logistics of the medal business. Most of the troops with whom I served had been overseas a long time, without any leaves home. The public may have the impression from the Vietnam war and overseas service since that time that military persons are given leaves to come home from time to time. Not so, in World War II. Transportation was by troop ship. It was slow and space was scarce. No one came home for a leave. We had songs about that. The people with whom I served had 48 continuous months overseas by the time we went home. Going home was supposed to be based on a point system, which was maintained in the Pentagon. A service man or woman received one point for each month served overseas. One received five points for each campaign. I think that I received three of those. One for New Britain Island, one for Luzon and one for the Visayan group, which consisted of Panay and Negros. One also received five points for each medal. This is the crux of my story. A medal was "money in the bank" in the going home marathon. I'll explain later why it didn't matter in the end.

Not until I started to think about writing this chapter did it occur to me that maybe these worthy Lt. Colonels had no real interest in the fate of the troops we were looking at, but were on a mission to garner five more points for themselves. It didn't even occur to me three years ago when I wrote an article for Emeritimes, our Retired and Emeritus Faculty newsletter about what the end of World War II was like for me. I wrote of these three officers and our flights, without thinking that they might have been using me to gain five points for themselves. I should get shot at three times for that? I might have been angry even as late as three years ago. Now, however, it is simply an amusing possibility. We shall assume that these three were deeply concerned over the positions of the troops below us, and that the awards of Bronze Stars were afterthoughts that occurred to their commanding officers. Why not look at it that way?

Chapter Thirty One

SOME COMBAT
THAT I DIDN'T SEE

L est the reader think that re-taking the Philippines was a cake walk, let me digress from my story and relate a story given to me by Major John Kriegsman, who was Division Artillery Air Officer of the 77th Infantry Division. All of this chapter is derived from conversations with John over many years, and a written summary he provided for me, when he discovered that I was about to "tell all."

John has now and had at the end of the war a good appreciation of the potential of the L-4 Liaison aircraft and Liaison Pilots in warfare. By the end of their campaigns, the commander of the 77th, General A. D. Bruce, shared this appreciation. He said: "The secret weapons of the South Pacific war were the Piper Cub and the bulldozer." A part of the story to follow will illustrate why he might think so.

I quote John Kriegsman's document here:

The bulldozer could clear the area for an

airfield in a matter of days. It could make a roadway in a matter of hours. Using their slave labor, it took weeks and months for the Japs to do the same thing. The Piper Cub airplane was an effective, efficient and cheap way to see into the jungles, trees and the hills before the roads were built.

When the 77th division loaded for the invasion of an island the Cubs had to be disassembled, and carefully loaded on the deck of a transport ship. At the landing area they had to be carefully unloaded onto a surging landing craft for the trip to the beach. The wings had to be replaced and the airplane test flown before observing could begin. A better part of a day could be used. Finding an uncluttered beach to use temporarily as an airstrip was also a problem.

This was the case July 27, 1944, when the 77th hit the beach on Guam. Actually by noon the Cubs were in the air observing, and directing artillery fire. By evening, they were able to direct the perimeter fires for protection during the night.

On October 20, 1944, General MacArthur made his famous return to the Philippines on the Island of Leyte. The 77th was in floating reserve, and brought on shore on November 21st. All equipment was made ready. Major air, sea and land battles were fought in the Leyte Gulf area. The U. S. Navy managed to cross the "T" in its battle with a Japanese fleet. The American Army drove the Japanese Army to the West over the mountains to the Ormoc Bay area where they hoped to be reinforced. U. S. Destroyers hastened to the Ormoc Bay area to stop any infiltration. On December 4th a major skirmish occurred between the destroyers and the Japanese bombers in which a couple of destroyers were sunk. December 5th I was dispatched to fly over Ormoc Bay to see if any activity was happening. There was none. I established a landing strip at Baybay for the 77th Air Sections.

On the late afternoon of December 6th, about 8,000 of the 77ths men loaded into small landing craft of all descriptions. Under cover of darkness they moved around the southern tip of Leyte to arrive at daybreak in Ormoc Bay behind the Japanese lines at a little fishing village called Desposito and Ipil which was ten miles south of Ormoc City, to disembark at 7:00 A.M. on the infamous day of December 7th... . Cubs from BayBay were already in the air covering the landings. General Bruce sent a message to General Hodges, Commander of the 24th Corps: "the 77th has landed. 7 come 11." A Cub delivered the message over the mountains in minutes. The 7th Infantry Division was coming up the coast from the South and the 11th Airborne Division was coming down the Ormoc Valley from the north of Ormoc City. About 40,000

Japanese were in the area. Fortunately they were in disarray from their trek over the mountain from the eastern shores. They were making an orderly retreat hoping for seven ships to arrive with reinforcements from Manila in time to help them.

One [Jap] transport did arrive at the Port of Ormoc City on Sunday night December 12th. ....When the unloading ramp was lowered and men began pouring out, all hell broke loose. In less than one hour only one soldier of approximately 750 remained alive. He was found a week later curled up in the "crow's nest." The other six transports were sunk the next day by U. S. Air Corps airplanes.

For the next week the fighting became a slaughter of the enemy. It took six days for two bulldozers to bury the dead. On Christmas Eve, 1944, another Combat Team from the 77th loaded on landing craft for an all night 'cruise' to Palompom on the west coast for a surprise landing on Christmas day. This was to prevent the escape of the remainder of the Japanese army on Leyte. The main street became a landing strip for the Cubs. They were the only link over land to Ormoc City. The road was still under control of the Japanese who could observe the road from their command post high in the hills.

During the week between Christmas and New Years the 77th, going North, was met by the 11th

Division coming South. The island was declared secured. The area was turned over to the Americal Division. They still found plenty of the enemy to deal with.

During this operation Cub surveillance was constant. Initially beaches were used as airstrips. As the Infantry occupied an area, the flat fields and roadways were established as airstrips. Cubs were constantly in the air; directing artillery fire, dropping rifle grenades, flushing the Japs out of buildings, hauling white stove gasoline to the Infantry units mired in mud, hauling out the wounded and the dead and delivering mail and blood plasma.

Immediately on January 1, 1945, the 77th Division moved back to the Eastern shore on the Gulf of Leyte to prepare for the next operation. OKINAWA!! We could not even pronounce the name. During the weeks that followed, we were constantly upgrading our equipment, getting supplies and training new recruits.

At first through the grapevine we heard that we were to secure a group of islands. It developed that they were near Okinawa, wherever that was. These were five islands which were huge piles of rock in a circle. The diameter of the circle was about two miles. It was a perfect anchorage for supply ships for the Okinawa operation. There were no beaches. (They were called the Kerama Rhetto Islands.)

About two weeks before we were to leave we found that we were going to leave Leyte a week before the main task force, to establish this anchorage. ...We were issued two of the craziest looking hooks we had ever seen ...to be mounted on our Cubs. We were to hook something, but we didn't know what it was. Somehow word came that we were to operate off of LST 776, which had a Brodie device on it, whatever that was. .... Several days passed, and the transport did arrive. Contact was made with the Commander. He was extremely vague. He was unable to supply a picture, or even a sketch of how the LST was fitted to hook a Cub, or why it was necessary in the first place. He did say that the LST was used at Iwo Jima by the Marines who had L-5 Stinson aircraft. They were much heavier than our Cubs. The Marines waited on board until an airstrip was secured on shore, then they took off, and never returned to the ship.

LST 776; Brodie device on port side.

LST 776 with the awkward Brodie device mounted on its deck did arrive late in the day. The convoy was to leave for these Kerama Rhetto Islands early next morning. Several of the 77th Air Section, including Lt. Montgomery and myself went on board. The crew told us how the device worked, and what we were expected to do to get our Cubs hooked on it. Next day the convoy assembled early to move out for the Kerama Rhetto Islands.

With the convoy under way we were the show of the day. All eyes and field glasses from nearby ships were on us as we gingerly flew around the LST valiantly trying to hook the loop. Lt. Montgomery was the first to hook the loop after only three passes. I managed after five passes. Thanks be to God we did not damage our precious planes (there was only room for two aboard the LST).

LST 776 was a strange looking craft, but very simple. Forward was a steel pole about 30 feet high. An arm protruded over the port side of the ship for about 30 feet, at about the 10 o'clock position. The same thing [was at the] aft of the ship, with the arm pointing about the 2 o'clock position. The ends of the arms had a cable going from one to the other, similar to a trolley cable. On the top of each end of the arms was a sort of receiving platform for the crew to stand on in order to manipulate the trolley.

An L-4 has hooked the nylon loop and is being slowed to a stop by Navy crewman.

To take off, a small nylon hook about 12 inches in diameter was installed in the small "eye" at the top of the hook [attached to the Cub]. The pilot, passenger and the Cub would be lifted up [with the engine running], hooked on the trolley, and transferred to the larger cable. The crew would pull the trolley aft as far as it could go. It would be held there while the LST headed, with full power, into the wind. The pilot would apply full throttle to develop maximum RPM for take-off. He then signaled when he was ready. The crew would release him.

The cable was about 300 feet long. When the pilot arrived at about the 3/4 point he pulled the "chain," much like flushing an old-fashioned toilet. He still might not have enough air speed, but he was free of the trolley. By using that 30 feet elevation, he could nose down to pick up enough airspeed just before he hit the water. From there on it was normal flying until it was time to land. We did not feel that it was a risky operation at all. We were concerned, however, about the lack of a chance to practice, since we were the only two Cubs that could observe the initial landings. We were led to believe that we were most important for the success of the whole operation.

When a plane was to land a trolley device would be rolled aft on the cable. A nylon rectangle about three feet wide and four feet long would be dropped from it. The LST would be turned into the wind at full speed. The LST had little or no keel. As a result, the ship would roll greatly. This meant that those arms out over the side would make an arc maybe 30 feet high. On the approach it was necessary for the pilot to get the rhythm of the ship in a sort of porpoise fashion, so that when he hooked the loop, or, worse yet, missed the loop, the arm would not come crashing down on him.

All Cubs were "taildraggers." When you made a three-point landing, you pulled the "joy-stick" into your belly. It was as natural as pulling on your trousers. NOT SO, when you hooked the loop. You had to remember to jam the stick ahead at the slightest tug hinting that you were hooked to keep the nose DOWN so the prop would not go up into the cable and get all chewed to pieces. The worst thing that could happen was to think that you were hooked when you were NOT, and you jammed the stick forward. Diving straight down could make a BIG problem (as you had only 30 feet to the water). Without any practice or instructions, this required extreme concentration

Securely hooked, the trolley with the Cub attached would roll down the cable. The ship's crew would stop the roll. At the forward end of the cable the crew would transfer the Cub to the cable going onto the deck of the LST and lower it to the deck.

An L-4 being lowered to the deck of an LST from the Brodie landing cable.
194

It was March 26, 1945. As the 77th Division convoy approached the Kerama Rhettos within about 30 miles, we took off to observe whatever we could see. There were very few houses, and no activity. Over our radio we were asked if we noticed anything unusual. We reported a funny thing. All the islands had railroad tracks going from the water into caves. Why? We could not figure it out. There were dozens of caves with the tracks, with nothing else around.

It turned out that this information probably was the greatest observation we ever made. Those caves contained small, fast boats with at least one depth charge loaded on each one. The Japs figured that an American task force might attack Okinawa. They did not believe anyone would even bother to look at the insignificant and rocky Kerama Rhettos. The area is dotted with such islands. Had they realized their importance to the American fleet, they could have easily camouflaged those railroad tracks and caves.

One of the caves housing the skiffs with depth charges. Kamikase type operators would drive them into the water and against the rubber of U.S. ships.

195

The Japanese plan for the use of these Kamikaze piloted boats was this. When the American convoys assembled to attack Okinawa under cover of darkness these small, rather fast boats would come like a swarm of bees. They would drive the boats into the rudders and propellers of the ships at anchor, rendering them easy prey for their bombers. The pilot of the boat had no chance of escaping before the considerably great explosion. ....With the discovery of these caves before any action could be taken, however, the destroyers protecting our small convoy immediately moved into positions of firing into the caves and destroying the boats and their lethal weapons. ....

In the course of the Kerama Rhetto operation tragedies did occur. Colonel Royal Gervais, second in command of the Division artillery, Combat Team Commander Colonel Lever and several other officers and men decided to investigate one of the caves, and maybe get a boat. As they approached the cave, they saw a couple of Jap soldiers run inside the cave. Whereupon, with drawn pistols, they all ran to catch them. They were bent on capturing those Japs alive for questioning. As they reached the cave, almost without caution, a terrific explosion occurred! The cave erupted like it was a huge cannon barrel. Colonel Lever was the first to arrive at the cave with others at his side. They caught the full blast! For about six of them, the war was over.

Each night during that week the 77th convoy would retire about 50 miles out to sea. In the anchorage they had little or no protection from anything that might happen during the night. The shores were so close to the anchorage and not necessarily secured yet. ....

As an LCVP (landing craft, vehicle and personnel) was hurriedly lifted from the water, a "pelican" which secured the boat to the cable snapped open on one end of the boat while it was in mid air. This caused one end of the boat to drop abruptly. At the same time the end that held shot upwards just as abruptly. A sailor was on that end riding it up to the mooring deck. He flew through the air. To break his fall, he grabbed the hoisting cable just as it was going over the elevator wheel. He managed to let loose of the cable, but his legs became entangled, and were crushed before the wheel could be stopped. When the wheel was reversed, he was removed. Both of his legs just dangled. He was carried to the table in the wardroom where sedatives were administered until a ship's doctor from another ship could be brought aboard. The next day he was transferred to a hospital ship.

That tragedy probably saved us from the tragedy that happened at sea. As a result of the delay, the convoy was out of sight, so we remained in the anchorage for the night. The convoy was attacked by a group of Kamakase planes based on Ie Shima as they sat in their rendezvous area. Several ships were hit. About 60 men were killed. One ship suffered the most casualties. A Kamikase managed a direct hit into the wardroom where the Admiral in command of the convoy, Combat Team Commander Colonel Tanzola, his S-1, his S-2, S-3 and about 40 other officers and men were killed or wounded. (The S-1 is the Executive Officer, the S-2 is the Intelligence Officer and the S-3 is the Operations Officer. Ed.) The S-4 (Supply Officer), Winthrop Rockefeller, who escaped being killed, was badly burned on his face and hands. He could have gone home, but he stayed on until he could be returned to duty.

About the fifth day of the Kerama Rhetto operation a landing strip was established on the Island of Zamemi. It was mostly deep sand. It had a flat area about the size of a city lot with a sort of grass growing on it. We could make our take-off roll on the hard surface. By the time we got to the really deep sand we would be light enough to pick up speed and almost roll out over the water.

The big problem was landing. The rough mountains (hills) being so close, we had to make our approach over the water in spite of the prevailing tail wind. When we landed we almost stopped dead in the deep sand. While it saved us from going into the hill, it presented a problem. With the stick in our belly, we could not move. If we released the stick (back pressure) too much, the wind would blow our tail up into the air. This happened once. Luckily the prop stopped crosswise, and did not get broken as the plane nosed over. That strip served as our base for the rest of the week.

I doubt that in their wildest dreams did the Japanese believe that 1400 ships would arrive during the night of March 31, 1945. They were ready for the assault on the beaches on April 1st. ... It was the greatest maneuvering of ships under cover of darkness that had ever happened up to that time. If there were collisions they were only very minor. It was an amazing feat, because the Captains of those ships were from all walks of life. They trained for this duty only short months before. The captain of our LST 776 was Lieutenant Copeland, a tobacco farmer from North Carolina. He died in about 1960.

Flying around the Kerama Rhettos ...all we could see in the direction of Okinawa, about 30 miles away, were a few battleships, cruisers, destroyers and mine sweepers cruising along the shores of Okinawa softening the beaches. They also hit Shuri Castle, a huge underground installation. Two days before the invasion "Long Tom" Artillery was placed on two very small atolls about two miles off of the point of Naha. We were called on to observe the firing of the Long Toms [heavy artillery]as they zeroed in on prepared targets in preparation for the landings the next day.

.... For the last time we flew off of our beloved LST 776, and landed at Kadena Airfield. LST 776 disappeared over the horizon, only to show up again for training purposes in Manila Harbor on Luzon Island in the Philippines.

Two new Stinson L-5 aircraft were issued to us. Each was equipped to carry a stretcher. They were loaded on a carrier at Ford Island in Hawaii. They were so insignificant compared to the exotic airplanes on the carrier that they were hung from the ceiling of the hangar deck. Captain Moen and Jim Hamlan were assigned to fly them to Okinawa when the carrier got anywhere near Okinawa. In the course of preparing them on the deck of the carrier, one was dropped. It was damaged so severely that it was necessary to push it overboard. When the carrier was about 150 miles from Okinawa they showed the two Liaison Pilots where Okinawa was on the map, gave them a compass heading and ordered them to take off.

Neither had been checked out in the heavier L-5. The instruments were bare necessities. It was not known whether the crude compass could even be trusted. So they flew for two hours over water before they even spotted land. They still had about one-half hour supply of fuel. They knew where the Jap airfields were on the map, but they were not sure who controlled them. All they had been told was that the Kadena Airfield had been captured by U. S. forces. They could see Jap airplanes all over it; they turned out to be dummy planes dispersed around the field. ...So they landed. This was one week after the 77th began its capture of the Kerama Rhettos

After Okinawa the 77th Division returned to Cebu Island in the Philippines for an R. & R. (rest and recuperation). It was to prepare for the next operation, which was to be the BIG ONE! A meeting was held in Manila for an evaluation of LST 776 with the Brodie Device. Would it be useful for the Kyushu (Japan) operation, which had huge cliffs at the invasion site? It would be a deadly reception!! Certainly this LST was the perfect solution for early observation. As a result, four more LST's with the Brodie device were ordered to be built. Fortunately, Hiroshima and Nagasaki solved the problem. .

I borrowed the above story by John Kriegsman because it contains experiences that are so different from my own. Also, it illustrates the flexibility of the Liaison aircraft and their pilots. The penultimate paragraph in John's story also shows the contrast between ignorant use of the aircraft and pilots and the very intelligent use of them by the 77th Division and its officers. Whoever was responsible for sending the two Liaison Pilots off, with 2 1/2 hours of fuel, 150 miles from the island they were supposed to find, should have been held accountable for his decision. The cruising speed of the L-5 was about 105 miles per hour, in spite of its 185 horsepower. It was built for slow flight and heavy lifting. Its instrumentation was scarcely more than that of the Cub. It did have a "turn and bank," but that's about the only difference. To first sight land when you have one half hour of fuel left must be frightening. And it was unnecessary. They could have ridden on the carrier until land was in sight. They had "generously" provided the Liaison Pilots with a map. Imagine the utility of a map while you are at sea with no land in sight. No one checked the accuracy of the magnetic compass. After being handled on several decks and stored in suspension from the ceiling, who could tell what distorting magnetic influences had been at work on the compass? A ten degree error in it would have caused a miss of Okinawa so great that it might not have been sighted. They traveled only 150 miles in two hours, at an airspeed of 105 miles per hour. That means that the head wind component they were fighting was at least 25 knots. What was the cross wind component? If it was in the same direction as a possible compass error, they would have been very far off. Even without a compass error, a cross wind component causing an error in their track of 10 degrees would have put them 26 miles off of their intended course in 150 miles. The Island of

Okinawa is about 30 miles long, north to south. The Kadena Airport, for which they were aiming, is about 6 miles from the southern end. So, an error to the left of 26 miles would have put them 20 miles south of the Island, with one half hour of fuel. Would they have been able to see it and recognize it?

How do you tell what the cross wind component is, when flying over water? Charles Lindbergh had a drift meter, something that no L-5 that I ever knew had. Lindbergh hit the Irish shore only about forty to fifty miles off in a long flight. He was a genius, as is recognized by anyone in aviation. The rest of us are not that good. Would not a familiarization flight of one or two hours been in order? How did the pilots know accurately the fuel consumption at various cruise power settings without flying the airplane? How did they know that the ship's officers knew its location in the Pacific accurately enough to give them a precise compass heading in the first place?

The dropping of one aircraft to its destruction was another mark of carelessness that was not characteristic of the 77th Division's handling. Even on the tricky deck and equipment of the Brodie-equipped LST 776, such things did not happen. The accident resulting in injury to the sailor had nothing to do with handling the Cubs on board. It involved handling an LCVP. The cavalier treatment of Liaison Pilots and their aircraft was also noted by my friend "Dutch" Schultz, in his story of flying in North Africa and Europe. Air Corps and Navy airfields would not let them land, in some cases.[18]

John Kriegsman's military career illustrates to me the professional devotion required to carry off a smooth Air Section operation under Army field conditions in combat. John was a Reserve Captain in the Horse-drawn Field Artillery in Illinois. He was also a private pilot. He was willing to take a "bust" to Staff Sergeant in order to fly Liaison aircraft for the Artillery. That was the rank of most Liaison Pilots in the beginning. By the time he got his military flight training, that policy had been changed. He retained his rank, and eventually became a Major. He was supplied with pilots who were Staff Sergeants, however. At one point the Artillery General wanted him to get rid of the Sergeants and get Lieutenants of Artillery as pilots. He persuaded the General that, since these were good pilots and good soldiers, he could get them qualified for commissions in the Artillery. He did so, and they were all commissioned Second Lieutenants. The story above illustrates how very effective his air section was.

John has made a return trip to the Philippines. He visited the old scenes on Leyte. There he found that Japanese citizens had returned and exhumed the bones of the many soldiers buried in the mass graves dug by U. S. bulldozers. They had cremated the remains, and they provided vials of ashes to Japanese families suffering losses of members during that campaign. This illustrates, among other things, the generosity of the Filipino people, to allow Japanese people to do this. It also illustrates the fact that the Japanese people have sentimental attachments, and that the brutality of their actions in World War II was a phenomenon of a military dominated by feudal minds more than a characteristic of the people.

John continues his interest in aviation, though he is not an active pilot. He conducts the family moving and storage business from Pekin, Illinois. He has served in the Illinois State Legislature, and as a Trustee of Illinois Wesleyan College. His own statement is: "I have sung in a choir for forty years, and no one has ever asked me to solo."

Chapter Thirty Two

WINDING DOWN

The Philippines campaigns were coming to an end for the 40th Infantry Division. We had returned to the Island of Panay. The airstrip was the section of paved road at Guimbal. The main elements of the Division were garrisoned in tents a few yards back from the coast line. The 503rd Parachute Combat Team was left behind on Negros Occidental to keep the Japanese troops from charging down from their mountain retreats and raiding the population. The Japanese food supplies must have gotten very low, even though they were constantly raiding homes and villages in the mountain areas. There was not enough population at the higher elevations to supply them with much food.

On Panay, I have recorded the menace that the few remaining Japanese troops posed to the population and to ourselves. We were not free of raids at night into our garrison area near the coast. In some way, they would manage to get all the way down from the mountains in small parties to bedevil us. Our Air Section was called on from time to time to fly patrolling missions to report on their positions and activities. I have reported on three

207

of those flights that I made in one afternoon.

As the fighting wound down, the local authorities saw less need for the services of the guerrilla forces that had been so instrumental in our capture of Panay without many losses. However, the difference between a guerrilla and a bandit grew less distinct. There were train robberies and other depredations not attributable to the Japs. The local aristocracy asked us to disarm the guerrillas. Remember, the society in the Philippines was at that time feudal; the guerrilla soldiers were peasants, though they were led by middle class officers. So, we had a "weapons turn in day". We couldn't believe that these forces had driven the Japs from cities with these home-made zip guns and rusty old weapons. The answer was that they hadn't. They were peasants, but they were not stupid. You wouldn't have expected them to turn in their good weapons, would you?

The troops of the 40th were heavily engaged in training. We knew what it was for. It was for the BIG ONE, the invasion of the Islands of Japan. Practice landings of troops and equipment were made on the beaches near our bivouac area daily. Equipment, clothing and all gear was inspected and readied. All of this was at a more leisurely pace than we would have had if we had been still in combat, however. We had our new L-4Js, and so it was easy to get them into shape. We had to be sure that we were proficient in the art of partially disassembling them and loading them on 2 1/2 ton trucks. We also had to be certain that our gear, consisting of tools, spare parts and radios would pack well. We still used the crates in which some of the older airplanes had come. We did not get crates with the new L-4Js; they stayed back at Tacloban.

I have told, in Chapter 3, of a chance meeting with a former college acquaintance while I was on New Britain Island. The reader will think that there are too many such coincidences in this tale. These meetings did occur, however unlikely they might be. While still on New Guinea, in the "repple depple," I ran into a man who had graduated from my high school in Shelton, Washington, the year after me, Paul Armstrong. He was in command of an Engineer Company that was stationed not far from us. In some manner that I do not recall, we were able to locate two other men from that little town (population about 3,000 at that time). A Bill Mallows, who had graduated one year before me, was a Corporal in the repple depple, and ended up in one of the units of the 40th. I simply do not remember the unit, or even the branch. We located another person, a Sergeant Will Jackson. He was from Shelton, and we knew him, though he had gone to a different high school. We all got together for a swim in the South Pacific.

While we were doing the staging for the invasion of Japan, who should come from Sixth Army Headquarters, but Captain Paul Armstrong. He was a member of a team whose task was to evaluate the 40th in terms of its readiness to undertake the invasion mission. He did not tell me, of course, what was the outcome of the evaluation. Years later, at a high school reunion, where we combined three classes for one reunion, due to the small size of the classes, he told me the result. We had been prepared. He also told me something that we had not known. Our mission was to have been the capture of an island in Tokyo's harbor, to set up a communication center. The estimated casualty rate for us was fifty percent. (Remember, the casualty rate for the Division was 12.8% for all of its Pacific operations up to that time.) We had a bad feeling about our mission, but we did not know what it was beyond being an invasion of some part of Japan.

While Paul was in our area, I felt that I should try to entertain him. There was an officers' club in Iloilo. First things first. I assume that there was an adequate noncom club. I also assume that the USO had recreational facilities for the men who were not noncoms. I did not know these things; I simply assumed that people of different ranks were provided with adequate facilities. We could not locate Sergeant Jackson, but I could find Corporal Mallows. I did not know of an adequate place to have a party except for one of the clubs. Paul and I would certainly not have been welcome in the noncom club. I invited some of our pilots, and we went to the officers' club. Bill wore a jacket to cover up his corporal's stripes, and all went well.

We were moderately busy staging for our assault on Japan. The troops were assaulting our beaches regularly in landing exercises. In the Air Section, we were waiting, with some anxiety, the coming of the Brodie Device equipped LST. The structure and operation of

210

the Device were described in the preceding chapter.

Here I shall attempt to recite a brief history of its development and use. I am indebted to Bill Stratton, President of the International Liaison Pilots and Aircraft association (ILPA) for the information.[19]

A First Lieutenant James Brodie of Army Artillery was aware of the German U Boat menace to our shipping on the Atlantic. The Civil Air Patrol did a good job within its range of the coast, but mid-Atlantic was dubbed "the American turkey-shoot" by the Germans. Lt. Brodie was also an Engineer. He devised a system of cables, hoists and loops somewhat like that described in the chapter preceding this one. It was supposed to be used on merchant vessels in the Atlantic. In fact, it was installed on a cargo vessel, the "City of Dalhart" in the Gulf of Mexico. Staff Sergeant Gregory of the U. S. Army Air Corps made some take-offs and landings on it with a Stinson L-5.

Long range patrols with Air Force B-24s became possible, eliminating the "turkey shoot" area. Interest in Jim's device lagged. The Office of Strategic Services (OSS), forerunner of the CIA, became interested in the device as a way to support beachhead landings. They took charge of it in early 1944 and accelerated its development at Fort Belvoir, Virginia. Lts. James Knox and W. G. Rhodes from the Artillery Liaison Pilot School at Fort Sill joined the effort. There was a device on land, using a 500 foot cable. When it was decided that the Navy would adopt it, LST 776 was chosen as the model vehicle. We have seen LST 776 before, in the preceding chapter. Brodie, Knox, Rhodes and Gregory all went to Coronado Strand, San Diego to perfect the device. The choice of the LST limited the cable length to 300 feet, as the LST's length was only 340 feet. This was compensated by the LST's ability to get under way and provide some head wind for the takeoffs and landings. It was complicated by the rolling motion of the LST. Only two L planes could be stored on the deck, so the observation load was heavy on the chosen two, although more pilots could be assigned to the mission.

The L-5 had an electric system and starting motor, so it could be started after attachment to the loop for takeoff. The L-4, on the other hand, had to be hand started on the deck before being hoisted. This was tricky for the Navy crew handling it. On several occasions when the idling engine died while in transit, the pilot would use the technique described in an earlier chapter of this story. There was a slight difference. There was no ground to stand on, so he stood on the right V of the landing gear, while the L-4 was swinging in the breeze, suspended by its hook from a nylon loop attached to a cable. Tricky business, but it was done several times.

LST 776 had not a very good experience with the Marines using the BRODIE device on Iwo Jima. We have recounted the success that it had with the 77th Infantry Division at Okinawa. It then went to Manila to be used in training crews for use in the invasion of Japan. That is where we came into the picture. Major Schuman, our Divarty Air Officer, went to Manila for the training. LST 776 was to be brought to Panay, so

212

that the rest of us could receive the training. I was vaguely aware of some such device, and not really eager to try it. We were "saved by the bell." The war ended before our education was complete in this respect.

Let me tell you how I learned of the happy news that it was over. I was on a mission by myself in my new L-4J, happily cranking the Robley propeller to new positions to see what kind of cruise I could get. I was really supposed to be checking on the Jap troops in the hills, to see whether they were behaving themselves. Though the war had been over for them for some time, they would not acknowledge it. They continued to be a nuisance. After an extremely dull flight, I was heading back to the airstrip at Guimbal with the negative intelligence that no activity could be observed. It really should have been good news, but we knew that, after dark, they would be up to some mischief. We did not fly after dark, and we would not have been able to see them, anyway. We did not have lights on our airstrip

I was listening to the Artillery net on the field radio installed on the rear deck. The news was broadcast that Japan had surrendered! The flight was no longer a dull one. This was the most exciting news of the whole war. As I approached the airstrip, I could see Infantry, Armored and Artillery still hitting the beach in a landing exercise. At mess that evening, I asked someone who was directly involved why they kept up the exercise. "The General's orders" was the response that I got. My observer said that the General then stood on the beach and cried. "For joy, just as I did," I replied. My observer said that that did not appear to be the case. The General was heard to say something like this: "There goes my chance to earn another star."

That General, the Division Commander, was a Brigadier General (one star) in a position that merited Major General rank (two stars). I am not using the name of this General. I have only this slender, hearsay evidence that he said anything like that. The reason that I am not more reticent about revealing this kind of sentiment is this General's subsequent behavior made it seem not unlikely that he would feel like that. Let us not take the report too seriously. His reputation among the men and officers was such as to lead us to believe a story like I had just heard. Let us assume the best, and conclude that the General met the war's end with mixed feelings.

My feelings were not mixed. I considered it a reprieve. I have mentioned before that we had foreboding feelings about our next mission. I only learned 30 years later how dangerous our mission really was to be. I later learned that the top brass of the Division did know about the nature of the mission. I don't know how far down the ladder of rank that information about our mission was shared. I now have mixed feelings about my own attitudes. When the A-bombs were dropped on Hiroshima and Nagasaki, I was glad. I believed, as did most people, that they would hasten the surrender of Japan. We all believed that many lives would be saved, Japanese lives as well as our own, by a hastening of the surrender. I still believe that that

214

is true.

The trouble is with the means; were they justified by even this salutary end? The world has been subjected to a great deal of second thoughts about the means. What was done at Hiroshima and Nagasaki would have been unthinkable a few years before. War does something to the human mind that is not good. I can recall, before we were in the war, seeing a Picasso original called "Guernica." It was hanging in the Widener Library of Harvard University. It is very large, abstract and garish. I had no idea what it was, but I was drawn to it. Looking at it for a few minutes, I became angry. The next time I was in the library, I looked at it again, with the same result. I was puzzled. I looked up its origin. It represented the bombing of the civilian population in the Spanish Basque city of Guernica by the Nazis. There was no military significance to Guernica; the purpose was to harm the morale of the population. Pablo Picasso knew what he was doing. He was skilled enough to evoke anger with an abstract painting. The world was indeed revolted by the bombing of civilian populations, but in just a few years, it became routine to bomb such places as London, Berlin, Frankfort and Dresden. These first three cities had some military significance, but the Dresden bombing was overtly done for its effect on civilian morale. The fact that the theory was wrong does not ameliorate the act of bombing for morale purposes.

A new element was introduced in Hiroshima and Nagasaki; the A-bomb was a terror of a different magnitude. President Truman was probably right in his

215

decision to drop the A-bomb. I am told that he received no contrary advice; all of his counselors agreed that it should be used. Many of us are not so sure now. In fact, it has in effect been outlawed. Any nation or group using it now would be branded a terrorist organization. Perhaps we have recovered some of the sanity that was lost in the "great war," or "The Good War," as Studs Terkel calls it.[20]

In the tales that I have told in this volume, the "good war" aspect of the fighting should come through. The war was not of our choosing. All that we were doing, in all theaters, was recovering territory that had been conquered by cruel masters. We felt good about our mission, though the details of fighting a war were odious. There is no instance that I can recall when the civilian populations that we encountered did not welcome us. We came close to being ignored in an area of the Tarlac Valley just north of Bamban, where we stayed for so long. North of that village, out in the valley, was a mountain called Arayat. On its slopes was located the headquarters of a group called Hukbalahap. They were communist in orientation. They not only disliked United States rule of the Philippines, but also disliked the national government of the islands. They did not oppose us; they did not help us, either.

216

Chapter Thirty Three

OCCUPATION

I have no recollection of our loading and shipping to South Korea. The first that I remember of it is our entry into the harbor of Inchon, the port city serving Seoul. We did not attempt to unload our equipment there. We did go into Seoul by rail and spend a few days there. We were quartered in Japanese-style houses and dormitories. The city seemed quaint, with its smoky soft-coal burning and the "honey wagons" making their rounds.

A railroad station in Yong Dong Po, near Seoul. South Korea.

We had been assigned the southern tip of the peninsula as our charge; to round up and ship home the Japanese military and civilian personnel still remaining in Korea. The plan apparently had been to ship us down the peninsula by rail. The train system was in a state of disarray, so we went back to Inchon and boarded the Navy vessels again. We made our way south along the coast through the Sea of Japan and into the Korea Strait. Some of these waters had been mined. Our forces knew very little about the pattern, so we forced the Japanese Navy to escort us. A phalanx of Japanese Navy vessels preceded us down the coastal waters. I saw no mine explosions; I simply do not know how many mines might have been swept or encountered on the trip. It was exciting, however, because of the idea of sailing through mined waters.

The Japanese Navy left us as we entered the harbor of Pusan. A smellier place would be hard to imagine. We discovered the source of much of the smell. Strange looking bales on the docks turned out to be night soil dried and packaged for shipment to Japan. One might define various degrees of exploitation of a conquered country, but taking their night soil home to fertilize the master nation's fields tops any concept that I have been able to come up with.

We were based at Masan, a Naval and Air Force training base for the Japanese. For a short time, however, we were at a training base for Kamikaze pilots. The airplanes were, understandably, quite worn out and rickety. What impressed us, though, was the mind

218

altering property of the sake that we found. We drank some of it, and it turned us into wild men. We didn't know what was added to it, but it would make tigers out of Walter Mittys

It was amazing to me to see how rapidly friendships developed between American soldiers and officers and their Japanese counterparts. I was standoffish toward them. However, several of our officers would go pheasant hunting in the hills with Japanese officers, each carrying one of the sport shotguns that we found at the base. I remember one incident in our quarters. About ten in the evening, here came a small Japanese Lieutenant carrying an American officer who was dead drunk. The American was the General's aide. This was not Captain Munyan, General Brush's Aide, whom I have met recently. Captain Munyan had contacted Dengue Fever and been returned home. We didn't have General Brush anymore, either. This was a young Lieutenant. The Japanese Lieutenant said something like: "He is my friend; please, where is his bed? I will put him on his bed."

The author in an abandoned airplane at a training field for Kamikaze pilots. You didn't need a paint job for their mission.

219

October and November came. The climate of South Korea results in some quite chilly nights and days in those months. We had our "summer" khakis and old fashioned fatigues for uniforms. We should have and expected to be issued wool uniforms. The word that we got was that a warehouse had burned, destroying our winter uniforms. We did not believe it. War and its vagaries give one an unduly cynical view of events. We did not actually see our uniforms on the street, but we believed that they had somehow made their way into the black market. I have since seen documentation of the supposed warehouse fire, so it must have been true that our uniforms were consumed by fire.[21]

HOW TO IRRITATE YOUR AIR OFFICER, PART II

Not long before going home from the tour in South Korea, the Major and I shared a routine mission. We were to fly back and forth along a stretch of the south Korean coast. A radar tracking outfit wanted a target to track, as a training exercise. I drew the first stint; I was to fly back and forth, just off of the coast for two hours. The Major would relieve me. At the end of the two hours, I had not heard from the Major. I was expecting a call on the radio saying that he was coming. He may have called me, but I did not hear it. I was sailing along, looking down at the coast. I glanced up, and there we were, head-to-head. Only the instant reflex that we had

220

been taught saved that coast line from being strewn with parts of cubs and pilots. We both turned hard right and passed very close to each other. The Major, and rightly, was irritated. He is the one who said that all you have to do is to fly one of those things long enough, and it will get you. Maybe he was right. I, too, was irritated. However, the Major had more right to be irritated. Remember, "rank has its privilege" RHIP.

We had arrived in September, 1945, and it was early in November when the orders came through for a lot of us to go home. The rush was due to factors that I shall detail later in this story.

Neither Fred Kutisch nor I had flown yet in November. In order to receive flight pay, each pilot must fly four hours in any month, or ten flights totaling three hours. On the day before we were to leave the unit, a severe wind was forecast. In the morning when we arrived at the airport, however, all was calm. We were at a Naval and Air Base at Masan, on the south shore of Korea. We had some auxiliary strips at various places nearby. Fred and I went to one of these strips. We made nine landings, and then flew around until almost three hours had elapsed. (Remember, we had only three hours of fuel. However, we did some slow flying to stretch the supply.) Then we headed back to Masan. Then the winds came. They were very strong, but they blew nearly straight down the runway at Masan. The stalling speed of the L-4 is 38 miles per hour. The wind was stronger than that. There was no way that we could make a three-point, full stall landing. After several tries, by landing on our wheels and attempting to come to rest in a three- point position, we found that we could not do it Any attempt to let our tail wheel down would result in our lifting off and being in danger of being blown against a building or other object. Sergeant Johnson, our excellent crew chief and Luigi, his assistant, stood on either side of the runway. As one of us would touch down with zero forward speed, they each would grab a wingtip and walk us into a hangar, after we cut power.

An excellent and ingenious solution. It did not do much for the irritation factor, however. The Major had one compensation. These two Lieutenants would be gone tomorrow. The Major was not going home. I am not sure, but it likely had something to do with the fact that his bride was still in the area.

The explanation came to us by rumor about why we were all going home at one time. Some of the officers and men had been overseas for 48 months. I had been overseas only 18 months. I did not have enough medals to make the difference. In fact, I had only the Air Medal with two Oak Leaf Clusters. The story was that the Division commander had received rotation orders for many of the men and officers and had put them on the shelf. His reasoning was that he needed experienced troops. For occupation duty? We had absolutely no prior experience in that type of duty. The story goes on to report that a Congressional investigation had resulted in orders for all of us with a certain amount of service or more would be sent home. I have never been able to verify that story. Anyway, we went home on Navy ships. There was very little air transport of troops in those days.

Chapter Thirty Four

EPILOGUE

I went into the separation center at Fort Lewis, Washington, determined to shake the dust of the Army from my boots and be a free spirit. Overseas and combat duty, if only for 18 months, leaves one with that kind of fatigue. The boredom and irritations of the experience were uppermost in my mind. Fortunately, cooler judgment prevailed. I came out the other side of the building a Reserve First Lieutenant in the United States Army. What had changed my mind? First, a twenty year retirement plan for Reserve duty was explained to me. I had already three years of Oregon National Guard duty, which would count, and nearly four years of World War duty. Not that far to go! A pension would not begin until age 60, but after completing 20 years of service, I could rest, or I could continue, earning more retirement pay and, if lucky, more rank. The clincher was that, with the Reserve duty, the Army would provide for flying time in Liaison-type aircraft; Taylorcrafts, Piper Cubs and Aeroncas, with which I was familiar. I would have to fly 80 hours per year to retain my proficiency and Liaison Pilot rating; a very reasonable requirement. Subsequent experience has taught me that 80 hours per year is the minimum that one should fly in order to be current.

I managed to maintain the rating, which was later changed to Army Aviator. I did not join an Aviation Company, but retained positions in Artillery Battalions. I became the Operations Officer of a Field Artillery Battalion in Lansing, Michigan. I earned the rank of Major in that assignment, while still maintaining my flying proficiency. I worked out an arrangement at the Pentagon so that Reserve Army Aviators could be attached to Army National Guard units for purposes of flying their Liaison aircraft. At that time the aircraft were Cessna L-19's, or "Bird dogs." They were developed during the Korean War, and were used there and in the Vietnam war. They were later designated the O-1, and the twin Cessna Skymaster was designated the O-2. I spent nearly four years with a Michigan army National Guard unit flying the L-19. When I left Michigan and arrived in the Los Angeles area, I found an opening for a Major as the Executive Officer of the 163 Combat Engineer Battalion, and thus completed my Reserve duty

ANOTHER LOSS

There is one loss of life that occurred after we were home and out of the active service. This was no less tragic, though it occurred shortly after the war and was only indirectly related to the war. Loren "Shorty" Froelich was a Lieutenant pilot, and a good one. He was the sort of fellow who was always the life of the party. His comments were the funniest and his antics were always amusing. He had very high spirits and he provided relief from some of our gloomiest moments. There was one problem about which we worried. He seemed to be a reckless flyer. He was not unskilled, but he took chances that most of us would avoid. He flew into more places, and he skirted more bad weather, and he landed in more awkward places than the rest of us did. I found evidence to support our fears in the 40th Division History.[22]

Shorty was awarded five Air Medals (one medal and four oak leaf clusters). None of the rest of us had been awarded more than three (one medal and two oak leaf clusters).

Shorty made it through combat missions unscathed, though there were bullet holes in his airplane. After we arrived in Korea, he began to suffer symptoms of Malaria. Aches and pains, fever, dizziness and ague are the symptoms. As I have said before, the Atabrine that we took did not prevent Malaria; it suppressed the symptoms. We were not aware of that fact; we thought that we were not getting Malaria. Enlisted men, all the way up to Master sergeant, were forced to take their Atabrine pills in the presence of a witness, usually in the chow line. Officers were trusted to take the daily pill. After arriving in Korea, where the Malaria threat was much reduced or not present, we were supposed to continue taking the Atabrine. Shorty, I think, grew careless about it. Anyway, he soon showed the symptoms that were suppressed in the rest of us. He was sent home and discharged from the Army.

On our way from the West Coast to the East coast, my wife Kathleen and I visited Shorty on his father's farm in Nebraska, where he was living with his wife and working the farm. Their child was on the way, and they were happily anticipating it. We heard soon afterward from his widow. A tractor had tipped over on him and he was killed. His widow said that she was trying to establish a service connection to his death, on the ground that he still showed symptoms of Malaria, which could well have caused the tractor accident. I did not learn whether she succeeded.

While in graduate school, in the winter and spring of 1946, I suffered aches and pains that I could not explain. I consulted a physician. He advised me to consult a Veterans' Administration physician. I did so and was examined. The answer that I got was that the symptoms were not service connected. That was not the question that I had asked. I wanted to know the cause and whether we could do anything about the aches and pains. I never did find out the nature of the illness, if it indeed was an illness. The symptoms gradually disappeared.

LIAISON AIRCRAFT AND PILOTS STILL FLY

Many years later, after years of flying for pleasure in

an Ercoupe and a Piper Cherokee, I became acquainted with the International Liaison Pilot and Aircraft Association (ILPA), based in San Antonio, Texas. It is headed by William Stratton, who started the revival of Liaison-type aircraft restoration and flying. Strangely, Bill was a bomber pilot in World War II. On starting a flight school after the war, he found that the training airplanes available were war-surplus L-2s, L-3s and L-4s (Taylorcrafts Aeroncas and Piper Cubs). He became fascinated by these versatile, spunky little airplanes and decided that others should share the fun. He spends a great deal of time keeping us informed and organized. ILPA's annual national convention is held in Keokuk, Iowa, on the weekend before the national Experimental Aircraft Association convention in Oshkosh, Wisconsin. A flight of "L-birds" then goes to Oshkosh and participates in the fly-bys preceding the daily air show there. There is an annual East Coast gathering of L-birds and an annual West Coast gathering. The second European gathering will be June 11, 12 and 13, 1999 at Middle Wallop Airport, near Winchester, England.

Bill Stratton, founder and President of the International Liaison Pilot and Aircraft Association

BIBLIOGRAPHY

1. Camozzi, Kenneth, Unpublished manuscript.
2. Cannon, Hardy C., Box Seat Over Hell, with research by William Stratton, San Antonio, Texas, Hardy C. Cannon, 1985.
3. Delk, James D., The Fighting Fortieth in War and Peace, Palm Springs, ETC Publications, 1998.
4. Eichelberger, Lt. General Robert L. and Milton Mackaye, Our Jungle Road to Tokyo, New York, Viking Press, 1950.
5. 40th Infantry Division,*The years of World War II,* Nashville, TN, The Battery Press, Inc., 1995 reprint.
6. Jones, James, WWII, New York, Crossett and Dunlap, 1975.
7. Morison, Samuel Eliot, The Liberation of the Philippines, Boston, Little Brown & Co., 1959.
8. Schultz, Alfred W., Janey, a Little Airplane in a Big War, Middletown, CT, Southfarm Press, 1998.
9. Steinberg, Rafael, Return to the Philippines, a volume of World War II, Time Life Books, Alexandria, Virginia.
10. Smith, Robert Ross, Triumph in the Philippines, Washington, D. C., Center of Military History, U. S. Army, 1984.
11 Stratton, William, Editor, Liaison Spoken Here, San Antonio, Texas, Fall, 1993.
12. Stratton, William, Unpublished revision of Hardy Cannon, Box Seat Over Hell, San Antonio Texas, 1998.

END NOTES:

1. Stratton, William, unpublished revision to Cannon, Hardy C., Box Seat Over Hell, San Antonio, TX, Hardy Cannon, 1985.

2. Schultz, Alfred W., Janey, a Little Plane in a Big War, Middletown, CT, Southfarm Press, 1998.

3. Cannon, Hardy C., Box Seat Over Hell, with research by William Stratton, San Antonio, TX, Hardy Cannon, 1985.

4. Steinberg, Rafael, Return to the Philippines, a volume of World War II, Time-Life Books, Alexandria, VA, p. 107.

5. Samuel Eliot Morison, The Liberation of the Philippines, Boston, Little, Brown & Company, 1959, p. 137.

6. Morison, Ibid., pp. 138-141.

7. Morison, Op. Cit.

8. Steinberg Rafael, Op. Cit., p. 109.

9. Morison, Op. Cit.

10. 40th Infantry Division, Nashville, TN, The Battery Press, Inc., 1995 reprint, p. 113.

11. Morison, Op. Cit

12. A. W. Schultz, Op. Cit., p. 217.

13. Jones, James, WWII, New York, Grosset & Dunlap, 1975, pp. 220-222.

14. Morison, Op. Cit., p. 229.

15. Ibid., p. 232.

16. Kenneth Camozzi, unpublished manuscript, 1998.

17. Jones, James, Op. Cit., p. 222.

18. 40th Infantry Division, Op. Cit., various pages.

19. Schultz, A. W. Op. Cit., p. 33.

20. Stratton, William, Editor, Liaison Spoken Here, Fall, 1993, pp. 1, 5, 7, 9 and 13.

21. Terkel, Studs, "The Good War," an Oral History of World War II, New York, Pantheon Books, 1984.

22. The 40th Infantry Division, Op. Cit., p. 150.

23. Ibid..